P9-CKX-681

Praise for SUPERFANS

"*Superfans* should be required reading for anyone wanting to build an authentic business that lasts forever. Platforms will change. Technology will change. But the one thing that will remain the same is that if you can help people and make them feel seen and heard, you're going to win. There's no one better qualified to talk about creating quality fans than Pat Flynn."
—**AMY PORTERFIELD**, host of *The Online Marketing Made Easy Podcast* and kombucha superfan

"One thing that has always stood out to me about Pat is just how devoted and loyal his fans are, and I'm excited to see him share his secrets in *Superfans* for all of us to learn from!"
—**LEWIS HOWES**, host of *The School of Greatness* podcast and superfan of salsa dancing

"Every business needs fans, but if you're ready to grow a massive business, I've seen first hand the impact that creating superfans can have on your bottom line. They are one of the most important assets for any brand, and in *Superfans* Pat breaks down exactly how to do it the smart way."
—**HAL ELROD**, international bestselling author of *The Miracle Morning* and *The Miracle Equation* and UFC superfan

"Everyone needs superfans to really succeed. Pat Flynn gives you powerful, actionable advice for how to attract the attention of your own greatest fans and gain their respect, admiration, and enthusiasm."
—**MICHAEL HYATT**, *New York Times* bestselling author and superfan of Blackberry Farm

"Finally! A book that breaks down what it means to build a true community! Navigating this space takes work as audiences become smarter at seeing through the noise. In *Superfans*, Pat Flynn sets you up to win big with your community, so that the moments you share will be more special and everyone in your tribe will say, 'He made that just for me.'"

—**AMY SCHMITTAUER LANDINO**, author of *Vlog Like a Boss*, creator of AmyTV, and superfan of Oprah Winfrey

"It's amazing how much value Pat packs into to all of this projects. And This book is no exception! *Superfans* is the winning formula for long-term business success. No matter where your followers are, the technology doesn't matter when you have superfans who will follow you anywhere. Read this book and you will have superfans who will share your message, and increase your influence and impact in the world."

—**SEAN CANNELL**, founder of Think Media, co-founder of Video Influencers, and superfan of Gary Vee

"For years I've been a student of Pat Flynn, watching him build an incredible business and community with some of the most passionate, loyal, and dedicated customers I've ever seen. In *Superfans*, he revels a step-by-step playbook to building a tribe of superfans, following the same secret strategies used by brands with the most passionate customers on the planet, including my personal favorite, LEGO. Buy this book, follow what Pat teaches, and transform your business (and your life) forever by building your very own tribe of superfans."

—**RYAN LEVESQUE**, Inc. 500 CEO and bestselling author of the books *Ask* and *Choose*, Adult Superfan of LEGO

"I have seen the future of marketing. And it is Pat Flynn."

—**MARK SCHAEFER**, author of *Marketing Rebellion* and Bruce Springsteen superfan

"I can't wait to use this book to connect my fans to one another AND to the show, because the snowball effect is real, and builds value for both the fans and the business itself."

—**JORDAN HARBINGER**, host of *The Jordan Harbinger Show* podcast and Will Smith superfan

"In *Superfans*, Pat unpacks one of the most important but often overlooked aspects of building a successful brand and business: creating, nurturing, and keeping raving fans. While everyone obsesses over how many followers they can get, Pat refocuses your attention on what matters more: how well you're taking care of the most faithful followers you already have. *Superfans* is a must read for any leader at any stage of business."

—**CHRISTY WRIGHT**, national bestselling author, host of the *Business Boutique Podcast*, and superfan of T.J. Maxx

"If you want your business to thrive, you need superfans. Grab Pat's book and study every word for a clear plan to develop ultra loyal fans."

—**MICHAEL STELZNER**, founder of Social Media Examiner and Social Media Marketing World, and *Star Wars* superfan

"In *Superfans*, Pat Flynn gives up his secret sauce. The answer to the massive success of the podcast, the products, and the people! If you've built a business, but wonder what makes the customers stick—and the revenue keep flowing—Superfans gives up the formula in actionable steps with practical relatable storytelling."

—**NICOLE WALTERS**, CEO and founder of Inherit Learning Company, and superfan of Amazon

"*Superfans* isn't just another business book. It's a book that can help you spark a movement. Creating your own superfans is the number one route to success in today's market where countless people are vying for your customer's attention. This book won't just help you to stand out, it will also lead you to more fulfilling work and making a bigger impact than you thought possible."

—**SHAWN STEVENSON**, bestselling author of *Sleep Smarter*, and superfan of the Marvel Cinematic Universe

"Lots of people talk about the importance of 'building an audience,' but no one tells you how. Just as importantly, no one has deconstructed how service is the real key to attracting long-term loyalty—until now. *Superfans* is refreshing, funny, and informative. After you read

it, you'll go away feeling motivated and ready to work. You might even find yourself looking around for the keys to your DeLorean."
—**CHRIS GUILLEBEAU**, author of *The $100 Startup*, host of Side Hustle School, and superfan of Peloton, OmniFocus, and Haruki Murakami

"If there's anyone who knows how to attract and build a tribe of loyal, raving fans using the internet, it's Pat Flynn! But, building a successful business doesn't stop at simply attracting customers. It's about serving them the right way, and for the right reasons. In his latest book, *Superfans*, Pat encapsulates all his experience into a manual that'll help you discover an easy and fun way to grow a business, stand out in your niche, and provide the solutions that your most valued fans and followers are clamouring for, more than ever before."
—**CHRIS DUCKER**, bestselling author and founder of Youpreneur. com, and Bruce Lee superfan

"I've accidentally seen the power of the superfan. Through sheer dumb luck, I've seen my business double twice over because of their impact. With Pat's book in hand, I will now set about doing it again . . . only this time with focus and a plan."
—**MICHAEL BUNGAY STAINER**, author of *Wall Street Journal* bestseller *The Coaching Habit* and superfan of Australian musician Paul Kelly

"Without raving fans, I wouldn't have been able to grow my brand (and Fire Nation!) to what it's become today. Pat breaks down exactly how anyone can create fans, systematically, but authentically, and *Superfans* is definitely a must-read for anyone who wants to become an Entrepreneur on Fire!"
—**JOHN LEE DUMAS**, host of the award winning podcast *Entrepreneurs on Fire*, and Providence College Friars superfan

"A powerfully practical manual for creating connections to your work, and to yourself. Packed with poignant stories and incredibly useful exercises, Superfans is the all-time best guide on taking your community from 'meh' to marvelous."

—**JAY BAER**, founder of Convince & Convert, co-author of *Talk Triggers*, and superfan of Radiohead and G4 tequila

"Pat Flynn lays out actionable steps to help readers understand how and why nurturing relationships elevates both your purpose and your bottom line. Learn how 'making it about them' is in fact the most natural way to develop die-hard fans of everything you do. Having superfans allows you to create better products and services, bring more joy to what you do and elevate your profits in the process. Honestly, even those who aren't in business will want to read this book because we all need superfans!"

—**CHALENE JOHNSON**, health and fitness expert, and superfan of all things reality TV

FOLLOWERS

SUBSCRIBERS

CUSTOMERS

VIEWERS

LISTENERS

READERS

FOLLOWERS

SUBSCRIBERS

CUSTOMERS

VIEWERS

LISTENERS

SUPERFANS

SUPERFANS

THE EASY WAY TO STAND OUT, GROW YOUR TRIBE, AND BUILD A SUCCESSFUL BUSINESS

PAT FLYNN

GET SMART BOOKS
SAN DIEGO
2019

Copyright © 2019 Flynndustries, LLC.

Published in the United States by Get Smart Books, a division of Flynndustries, LLC.

All rights reserved.

No part of this publication may be reproduced, distributed, or transmitted in any form or by any means, including, but not limited to, photocopying, recording, or other electronic or mechanical methods, without the prior written permission of the publisher, except in the case of brief quotations embodied in critical reviews and certain other noncommercial uses permitted by copyright law. For permission requests, write to the publisher at "Attention: Permissions Coordinator," at the address below.

8910 University Center Lane
Suite 400
San Diego, CA 92122
pat@smartpassiveincome.com

Important Disclaimer

This publication contains materials designed to assist readers in evaluating the merits of business ideas for education purposes only. While the publisher and author have made every attempt to verify that the information provided in this book is correct and up to date, the publisher and author assume no responsibility for any error, inaccuracy, or omission.

The advice, examples, and strategies contained herein are not suitable for every situation. The materials contained herein are not intended to represent or guarantee you will achieve your desired results, and the publisher and author make no such guarantee. Neither the publisher nor author shall be liable for damages arising therefrom. Success is determined by a number of factors beyond the control of the publisher and author including, but not limited to, market conditions, the capital on hand, effort levels, and time. You understand every business idea carries an inherent risk of capital loss and failure.

This book is not intended for use as a source of legal or financial advice. Evaluating and launching a business involves complex legal and financial issues. You should always retain competent legal and financial professionals to provide guidance in evaluating and pursuing a specific business idea.

Ordering Information

Quantity sales. Special discounts are available on quantity purchases by corporations, associations, and others. For details, contact the publisher at the address above.

ISBN 978-1-949709-46-9: Hardback
ISBN 978-0-9970823-6-4: Ebook

Categories: 1. Business Communication 2. Customer Relations 3. Marketing

Printed in the United States of America.

First Edition

THE FREE SUPERFANS BONUS COMPANION COURSE

To help guide you through *Superfans*, I created a free bonus companion course that includes downloadable worksheets, bonus video content, and all the resources and links mentioned in this book. This is your first step toward success with the content in this book, so I highly recommend you sign up now. The supplemental materials in this free course are organized by the sections and chapters of this book, making it easy for you to find what you need as you read along.

See you on the inside!

Visit the following link to get free access to your Superfans bonus materials now:

yoursuperfans.com/step1

This book is dedicated to Team Flynn, the amazing army of supporters who follow my journey. You've trumpeted my work, defended me from trolls, and you continue to proudly fly the Team Flynn banner high. I am forever grateful. Here's to you and your future superfans!

CONTENTS

PROLOGUE

I was unsure of what to expect, and quite frankly, a little scared of what my wife, April, was about to show me.

During dinner, we'd had one of our usual conversations about what life was like back in high school—way back before getting married and having kids. We attended the same high school and had the same circle of friends, so it was always fun to travel back to the past and talk about how weird we used to be and the stuff we used to enjoy.

We talked about the food we used to eat: In-N-Out Burger, cajun fries with meat and cheese at school, and of course, Filipino food at home.

We talked about the shows we used to watch: *Saved by the Bell*, *Animaniacs*, and *Total Request Live* on MTV.

And naturally, we always discussed the music we loved.

The nineties was an interesting decade for music. Nirvana bloomed, Green Day came around, and Britney Spears was always on the radio to hit us one more time. I loved all kinds of music, from Snoop Dogg to Blink-182, and I even had a single mixtape that included Gwen Stefani, Sir Mix-a-Lot, Incubus, and Linkin Park.

For April, though, there is only one band in her life that matters: the Backstreet Boys.

Or as she likes to call them . . . her boys.

I always knew she had a love for this group. She had all of their albums on CD, went to their concerts, and even had pictures of them in her school binder. But I had no idea about the true extent of her fandom until that evening when, after dinner, she said the words you don't want to hear after talking about the Backstreet Boys with your significant other:

"I have something I need to show you."

Immediately, I started to imagine a tattoo, one that, when certain muscles were flexed, all of the boys would do a little dance or something.

Thankfully, it wasn't that.

It was, however, something almost as surprising.

April went into the closet and took out a large opaque plastic bin and placed it on the floor. It looked heavy. Sitting criss-cross style behind it, she asked me, "Are you sure you want to see?"

Reluctantly, I said yes. How could I say no at this point?

Slowly, she removed the lid, and I immediately locked eyes with one of the band members staring right at me. It was the tall, blue-eyed, blonde member of the popular boy band, Nick Carter, on the cover of his 2001 calendar. He had a smoldering look, as if he were saying, "Hey, April. It's good to see you again. I'm still here. And who's *this* dude?" pointing at me.

I'm short and have brown eyes and black hair, the polar opposite of Nick Carter.

Underneath the calendar was a stack of programs from concerts. And then, I saw something I didn't even know existed: Backstreet Boys action figures, unopened. Five of them. One for each band member.

But wait. There's more . . .

Magazines, envelopes with who knows what in them, and then the clincher: a framed picture of Nick Carter.

I had seen enough. I knew from that point forward that April wasn't just a fan of the Backstreet Boys. She was (and still is) a *superfan.*

But little did I realize, April's hyperfandom for the Backstreet Boys, and the stories I later learned about how this all came to be, would be vital in helping me learn how to build a successful multimillion-dollar business of my own with superfans all around the world.

Actually, let me rephrase that:

April's superfan journey taught me how to build a successful multimillion-dollar, future-proof business **by creating my own superfans around the world.**

I don't have any hit songs or platinum albums. I don't have my own action figure, and I definitely don't have my own calendar.

I do, however, have a thriving business that is a result of the superfans who stand behind it. When I post about a location where I'll be, I can guarantee that I'll shake the hands of some of my superfans when I get there. When I share that I have a new product coming out, I'll have a waitlist of sometimes thousands of superfans who want to be the first to get their hands on it. And when trolls or bullies enter the community to flex, it's the superfans who show them the way out.

Fans are important, but superfans are everything.

Everyone is a fan of something, but if you're a superfan, you behave a little differently. To outsiders, your actions may seem ridiculous. You'll drive two hundred miles just to see your favorite singer. You'll buy anything and everything related to your favorite movie franchise. You'll spend countless hours during the week actively engaged in discussions in Facebook Groups or on Reddit, passionately defending your fan theories against someone else's. You'll tirelessly collect your favorite band's memorabilia and store it in a box in your closet for a decade to one day torture your future spouse.

As a superfan, you also become a hardcore ambassador for the object of your fandom. You wave that flag high, and you wave it proud. You tell your friends and family about it, even if they don't want to hear it. You take pictures and immediately share them on social media. You might even start a YouTube channel or a podcast about it, and over time, you'll influence even more people to start loving this thing.

Superfans invest time, money, and, most importantly, emotion into what they love. When the team wins, superfans feel like they've won, too. When the team loses, it's a tragedy. Either way, a superfan is very likely to shed a few tears. A superfan is a stakeholder—the most important kind.

It's common to think that superfans only exist for people or entities like musicians, movie franchises, and sports teams. It's what we see out in the wild. But what we don't see are the superfans of the many micro-worlds that exist around us.

For example, there's LEGO. Lots of people love LEGO, but the company has a big subset of superfans made up of people from all walks of life. This timeless and classic toy that lets people bring almost any vision to life has also inspired a dedicated fan community that includes Adult Fans of LEGO (AFOL), who attend meetings and conferences together. In fact, as you'll hear about in chapter 7, it was LEGO's superfans who helped rescue it from bankruptcy. They literally saved the company.

Or take California's own In-N-Out Burger, which has earned the superfandom of many because of its consistently delicious food (and its "secret menu" that makes those fans feel like insiders). The company also draws intense admiration for paying its employees higher than market rates, as well as the fact that it's still owned by its founding family and hasn't watered down the brand with franchising or going public.

There's also Harley Davidson. The motorcycle brand has a famously raving group of fans who resonate with its message of authenticity, freedom, and self-expression. The company hosts events around the country through the Harley Owners Group (HOG) that draws thousands of people and brings a special kind of energy to the fanbase. Those fans show off their brand loyalty through apparel—shirts and hats and jackets—and even their tattoos.

If you're trying to build a brand and a following, whether you're a business owner, artist, musician, YouTuber, blogger, podcaster, or creative of any type, superfans are the electricity that will spark your growth and the lifeblood that will keep your business energized. Your superfans have special powers and abilities that can support your mission, and that's what makes them super. When you build a tribe of superfans, you're building a future-proof brand that will allow you to succeed, no matter what the business or technological environment looks like.

Running a business means having your hands in multiple pies, from strategy to marketing to finance to hiring to much more. But focusing on the experiences that create superfans is more important than any other activity in your business. It's more important than getting more traffic, more followers, more views, or more subscribers. It's even more important than building your email list and acquiring more customers.

Why?

Because when you focus on creating superfans, as a byproduct you'll get more traffic, more followers, more views, and more subscribers. You'll build a stronger, more targeted tribe who will go out of their way to support you and what you do. They'll be more engaged, more excited, and more likely to take action. And they'll be more likely to buy from you, too!

Superfans are truly the life of your business.

Unfortunately, most businesses don't focus their efforts on building superfans. Yes, you can build a successful business without them, but you'll be spending a lot more time and money trying to get more people to find you—and even if they do, there's no guarantee that they'll ever come back. Plus, you'll leave yourself susceptible to algorithm changes, savvy competitors, and even hackers, any of which could crumble your business overnight. I've seen it happen over and over again, and it's never pretty.

Build a set of superfans, and no matter what happens, they'll always be there for you.

Instead of spending money on ads, spend more time on people. Instead of worrying about the latest growth hacks and strategies, worry about identifying and addressing the biggest pains and problems in your target audience. Instead of figuring out how to optimize your conversion rates, figure out the rate at which you're able to connect authentically with your audience and make them feel special.

Don't get me wrong. It's important to focus on things like building traffic and improving conversion rates, but unless the experience you offer your audience is infused with the magic that will help you generate superfans, all you're doing is working hard and spending time and money to show people there's nothing there that actually makes them feel *special*—nothing that makes them want to come back.

And no one is a superfan of anything that doesn't make them feel special.

Superfans exist at the top of something I like to call the **Pyramid of Fandom**. They're the smallest portion of your audience, but they're the biggest catalysts for your brand and the beating heart of your business.

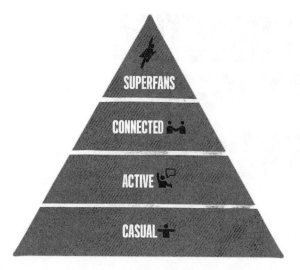

You'll be seeing a lot more of the Pyramid of Fandom in this book, as we explore the strategies and tactics to bring the people in your audience from casual to engaged to active to true superfans.

April's Backstreet Boys fandom may have been ignited the night she lay in her room trying to mend her heartbreak, but it didn't *start* that night. She didn't become a superfan because of that one song in that one moment. She became a superfan because of the many, many moments of hearing the band, seeing them on TV, talking about them with her friends, and yes, staring at Nick Carter's sultry gaze and cascading blonde locks on the March page of his 2001 calendar.

And in the same way, your very own superfans will join you not because of a single, huge magical moment, but because of those many smaller magical moments.

Whether you're a shy YouTuber just starting out, or the leader of a Fortune 500 company, your superfans are out there waiting for you to connect with them. You just need to create that journey, to pave the yellow-brick road that will guide them surely and steadily to superfandom.

Now I want to tell you a story about my *first* very own superfan.

INTRODUCTION: THE SUPERFAN PARADIGM

The year 2008 was a whirlwind for me. In February, I was promoted to job captain at the architecture firm I was working for, and in March, I asked April (my wife, not the month) to marry me, despite my being more of an N'Sync fan. Those were major life-changing moments, but the biggest life-changing moment came just a few months later when, on June 17, I was invited into my boss's office and was let go from my job.

The US economy was seeing record lows, and so was I. I fell into a state of depression trying to figure things out, especially related to April and our future together. I moved back to San Diego to live with my parents, and before committing to wait out the storm or go back to school to get my graduate degree in architecture, I randomly stumbled upon a podcast that would eventually change the course of my life forever.

The *Internet Business Mastery Podcast*, hosted by Jason Van Orden and Jeremy Frandsen, planted the idea in my head that I could potentially create a small business of my own on the internet. I began to obsess over the thought of being my own boss, almost as much as I obsessed over anything and everything Jason and Jeremy produced. I binge listened to their show for three to four hours a day. After each episode, I felt energized and inspired, and my mind raced as I brainstormed potential ideas for businesses that I could create. I eventually listened to all 150 episodes available in their archive—twice—and I invested in one of their online courses to help walk me through the process of building a website and an online brand.

Even though I had never met Jason or Jeremy, I was turning into a superfan. This became more apparent when I heard on an episode that Jeremy had decided to move to San Diego, and I actually cried after a sudden rush of excitement poured over me. This was the first time I'd really felt like a raving fan of something that wasn't mainstream, like a musician or a sports team.

A few weeks after that announcement, I was sitting down with Jeremy at a café, having coffee with him and a few other fans of the show, which nearly didn't happen because I almost chickened out and turned around on the way there. After introductions and a little fanboying, I found myself in what was a formally structured roundtable discussion called a mastermind group. I'd heard Jason and Jeremy talk about them on the show, but this was my first time ever being a part of one.

Each person got a chance to speak for about fifteen minutes about what they were up to and ask the rest of the group what they might need help with. I had never been so nervous in my life. I didn't have anything that felt like a real business to talk about, just a crappy-looking website I'd built to help people pass the LEED exam, a specialized exam within the architecture and design industry. It was making only $5-15 a day from advertisements. Not enough to live on, and definitely not anything I was super proud to share with the rest of the group, especially after hearing what some of the other people had to say.

There was a copywriter who was making upwards of $5,000 per client, a fitness expert who was creating and selling online courses, and an author who had a couple of best-selling books. I definitely felt out of place, so when it was my turn to speak, I wanted it to be over as soon as possible so I could hear everyone else, and more of Jeremy's magic.

But once I started telling the group the story of the LEED exam site I'd built to help others taking the test, the feedback they shared quickly gave me an entirely different perspective on what I was doing—and what was possible. When the group heard how much traffic my site was getting—upward of 5,000 visitors per day—they were flabbergasted. And when they heard I wasn't doing anything beyond advertisements to monetize the site, they were even more excited to point me in the right direction.

"Pat!" I remember Jeremy himself exclaiming. "You have to create an ebook and sell it on your site!" And he was right. I had a golden opportunity to create a passive income stream using the information and readership I'd built.

So later that night, I went home and started on my ebook. It took a few weeks of late nights to put it together, but within a day of posting it, I had my first sale. I was in business! I had a customer, and it felt awesome.[1]

And it would take only a few months before I had my first superfan.

Jackie and the Super 1,000

In December 2008, just a few months after launching my first product, I received an email from Jackie, a customer who had recently purchased my exam guide:

> Pat! I needed to write this email to you to let you know just how much you've helped me! First of all, thank you for your LEED Exam Walkthrough, I passed my test with flying colors just a couple of weeks ago and since then, I've been able to get a raise and a promotion at my firm! It was long overdue, but it was passing the exam that finally made it happen.
>
> Thanks to this raise, my family and I are able to plan a trip this summer to California to visit Disneyland. I know you're in Southern California, would it be possible for us to take you out to dinner? If not I understand, you don't even know me, HAHA! But, I just wanted

---

[1] You can find all the details of my mastermind turning-point story in my book Let Go.

> to say thank you for what you do. I'm going to tell
> everyone in my office about you and your guide and
> make sure everyone who is studying for the exam gets
> it. It's the least I can do. Let me know about Disneyland
> in the summer.
>
> From your biggest fan, Jackie

Your biggest fan? I had a . . . fan? For helping someone pass an exam? This didn't make any sense to me at first, but it was obvious this wasn't just one of those "nice things you say to someone." She actually wanted to take me out to dinner, and even share my guide with her entire firm. Again, for helping a person pass an exam.

Jackie and I swapped a few more emails, and unfortunately the timing didn't work out for our dinner meeting. But she represented my first encounter with a true superfan of my work, and I was able to experience the power that a single superfan could have in my business. My business grew to over six figures in earnings within a year after selling my first product, and this was all before I'd even started to build an email list! Imagine a tribe of just ten Jackies, or a hundred, or maybe even a thousand! A business can grow exponentially thanks to the power of a few, which is why when it comes to building a successful brand, you don't need millions of fans like Taylor Swift or Dwayne "The Rock" Johnson. All you need to shoot for is your *super 1,000.*

As I was starting my business in late 2008, I came across an essay called "1,000 True Fans" written by Kevin Kelly, senior editor at *Wired.* This masterpiece, which is still just as useful today as it was back then, was vital in helping me understand how achievable real, life-changing success actually was, and why I wasn't crazy for wanting to build a business in a super small niche (LEED exam prep).

His thesis was this: If you had just one thousand true fans (which he defines as "a fan that will buy anything you produce") and each of those true fans provided $100 profit per year on your art, your craft, your work, well, there's your six-figure business right there! Here's Kelly's longer description of what true fans are and what they're willing to do out of love for you:

"They will drive two hundred miles to see you sing. They will buy the super deluxe re-issued hi-res box set of your stuff even though they have the low-res version. They have a Google Alert set for your name. They bookmark the eBay page where your out-of-print editions show up. They come to your openings. They have you sign their copies. They buy the t-shirt, and the mug, and the hat. They can't wait till you issue your next work. They are true fans."

Sounds a lot like a superfan, huh? In fact, Kelly uses the term "super fan" interchangeably with "true fan" in his essay.

Back to those numbers. One thousand fans times $100 is $100,000. Obviously, that figure is before taxes, and there's a lot of other things to consider that would affect the actual bottom line, but his point still hits home: "Instead of trying to reach the narrow and unlikely peaks of platinum bestseller hits, blockbusters, and celebrity status, you can aim for direct connection with a thousand true fans." Or, the way I like to put it:

You don't need to change the entire world to build a successful business; you just need to change someone's world.

If you're new to business, this should be reassuring. This is achievable. To add even more perspective, that's one single fan each day for less than three years. No matter what niche you're in, there are one thousand people in this world who can potentially see you as their favorite. It's not going to take one thousand days, though, because as you probably already know, superfans tell everybody, and some of the people they tell will become superfans, too.

If you already have an established business and you're looking to grow and scale up, this should be exciting. Imagine a team of superfans who keep coming back, not just with more purchases, but also with more people.

And $100 per year? That's on the low end of what a superfan might spend with you. I know many people who pay $100 per month for things they don't even care about that much, like cable television or a subscription that they're just too lazy to cancel. But superfans? They'll go all out, and you'll see their impact on your bottom line.

"But Pat," you may be thinking, "I need a huge audience for my business to be successful, and you already have thousands of superfans…" Well, I want to tell you what having just one—yes, *one*—superfan can do you for your business.

A few months after my first conversation with Jackie, I got another email from her. She kept me up to date on her job, and she also let me know that she was able to make my website, GreenExamAcademy.com, a recommended resource within an internal advanced education program for her firm. I checked my database and confirmed that over twenty-five people from the same firm, which had multiple locations worldwide, had purchased my guide. And over the course of the next five years, I randomly saw sales come in from more people in the same firm.

That's what superfans do. They love and appreciate who you are and what you do so much that they're willing to go to bat for you, and recommend you to others unreservedly. They're the kind of fans who will help you make your business future-proof.

I want to help you find and cultivate raving fans who will bring *unexpected multipliers* into your business—like Jackie and the twenty-five others who became my customers because of her—and that's what this book will show you how to do.

A common question I get when I present the superfan journey is this: how many fans do I really need? The answer: Not as many as you might think. Remember, because of Jackie, at least twenty-five other people bought my LEED exam study guide. If you have just a few Jackies in your audience, someone who can inspire twenty-five other people to act on your behalf, then you're well on your way. And you can take comfort even if you're at the very beginning of creating your own audience of superfans, because quality (of fandom) is way more important than quantity (of fans). And yes, the fact that you can build superfans for something as unexciting as an architecture study guide should tell you that the same is possible for you, no matter your niche!

So where do you start if you want to cultivate your own legion of superfans that will follow you everywhere? We're going to begin at the bottom of the pyramid and work our way up, starting with how to convert your casual audience members—people who were recently introduced to you for the first time—into your active audience. As you read the next few chapters about the superfan journey, I want you to imagine the people in your brand and the experiences that you'll create for them. Again, you don't have to do all of these things to make an impact; think of it like a fun list of ingredients that you can pick from to create your own special cocktail of an experience, one that fits your style and taste, and one you can have fun doing!

For now let's take a closer look at the superfan journey and the most important principle behind developing superfans for your brand.

The Superfan Journey

I was at a business conference a few years ago, and the speaker on stage was talking about how to get noticed in the noisy world we live in so that we can attract more customers and build a more successful business. He offered us a thought experiment:

> "Imagine walking down the sidewalk, minding your own business, and then you see a nickel on the ground. And for you superstitious folks in the audience, it does happen to be facing heads up. Honestly, how many of you in this room would stop walking and pick up the nickel? Please raise your hand."

Would you stop to pick it up? In the room of around 250 people, only about 10 percent raised their hand.

> "Now, imagine walking down the sidewalk, minding your own business, and then you see a quarter on the ground. Also heads up. How many of you would now stop walking and pick up the quarter? Please raise your hand."

A lot more hands went up this time, about 40 percent of the room.

> "And finally, what if you came across a dollar bill lying
> on the ground?"

Now, most of the room raised their hand, although one person shouted that it might be a prank, which was pretty funny.

The speaker said that as we build our businesses, we should try to be like that dollar bill, which has two things working in its favor. First, it's something we don't normally come across, so it captures our attention. And second, it has immediate value, so we know it will be worth a person's time to stop and pick it up. If you want to win, capture people's attention and show them quickly how you can add value to their lives.

On the mean corners of Business Ave., there's a wealth of cheap coins on the sidewalk that we pass over and ignore, and other coins that we may see but aren't worth our time. And I like this analogy, but there's one big problem I have with it: capturing attention and adding more value is not enough. It's the minimum.

The phrase "add more value" has become an overused, default, borderline-meaningless answer to almost every "How do I build a successful business?" question out there:

> How do I get more subscribers? *Add more value.*
>
> How do I get more people to share my content?
> *Add more value.*
>
> How do I get better search engine results?
> *Add more value.*

Adding more value is the mandatory baseline. If you don't offer value, then you're not going to get picked up.

Let's continue the timeline of this thought experiment:

Imagine you find a dollar bill on the ground and you pick it up, and thankfully, it's not a prank. You put it in your pocket and carry on with your day. How many times during the rest of the day are you likely to think about that dollar bill? How often are you going to pull out that dollar bill and show it to your friends and family? And, if you were to lose that dollar bill, would it ruin your day? Would it change your life? Probably not.

Now, you could argue with me and say, "Pat, a single dollar isn't life changing, but if I found $10,000 on the ground, then it would be a different story. I would think about that all day, I would share it with people who are close to me, and I would feel terrible if it were suddenly taken away from me."

That's a valid argument, but here's the truth: It's not the money itself that you'd think about—it's the possibilities of what that money could do for you. The experiences and opportunities it could create for you. The ability to unlock something new in your life.

And that's the secret when it comes to creating superfans: to create new experiences and help audiences unlock something new in their life. Not only will you be found, and not only will people understand the value you have to offer, but they'll feel different as a result. They'll feel special. And that, in turn, will help them become your superfans.

When you become a superfan of something, it's not because of a person, a product, a name, or a brand. You become a superfan because of how that person, product, or brand makes you *feel*.

> # People don't become superfans the moment they find you. They become superfans because of the magical moments you create for them over time.

But how exactly do you create those moments, and what do they look like? That *superfan journey*, and all the methods and details you'll need to create it, is what we'll be exploring in this book.

Right now, though, I want to give you an idea of what to expect from the highest level, and for that we'll need to return to the Pyramid of Fandom.

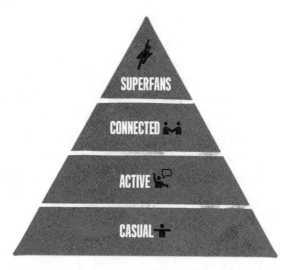

The entire Pyramid of Fandom represents the total number of people who know about your brand. Creating superfans is all about executing strategies that will take a person from each stage to the next, from casual to active to connected to the top of the pyramid: superfan.

Your **casual audience** makes up the largest segment of your audience. These are the people who don't find you because they know you, but rather via a recommendation, a link or mention on another website, a search result, a related video, or something along those lines. They are usually there because you've provided something useful, and they are there to get an answer or do a little research before either sticking around or leaving to find answers elsewhere. In terms of numbers, these people represent a majority of your view count or traffic, and many businesses, unfortunately, aim for that alone. People in this bucket are far from superfan status, and so at this early stage in the journey, your goal is to create a trigger that allows them to understand that they are indeed in the right place. That there's something special for them. That they should convert and become a part of your active audience, so they'll continue to come back.

Your **active audience** is the group who knows who you are and what you and your brand have to offer. When you share, create, or publish something new, your active audience makes a decision as to whether or not to invest time or money (or both) in that new content or product.

They are active members of the tribe who will take action and speak up, but it may take some convincing to do so. They live in your email list and on social media. They've taken action and at one point made a decision that they want more from you, which is a great start. But, they're still a ways away from the top of the pyramid. Next, you'll have to work to convert your active audience to members of your connected community.

Your **connected community** is where the magic starts to happen in your brand. Not only are you able to communicate regularly and easily with this segment of your audience, but they are also having conversations with each other. Community members begin to identify with the group and one another so much that they may even create a name for themselves. This is where a majority of your comments, feedback, and survey results will come from, and when it comes to creating anything new, the community becomes an essential asset for seeding and validating new ideas that can help the business excel and grow. And it's from this community that you build your brand's superfans.

The journey from the bottom of this pyramid to the top isn't easy. It's a climb, and it takes time. It requires patience, and it requires being hands on. But that's exactly why it works so well, because most businesses (not yours) aren't going to do this. Most businesses have the pyramid flipped, like this:

This inverted pyramid is what is known as a sales funnel, and it's the business model that most people aim for. It's easy to understand, it's relatively easy to create, and it's extremely easy to measure. People enter the funnel from the top, and a certain percentage of those people will become subscribers. A certain percentage of subscribers will see an offer on a sales page, and a certain percentage of those people turn into paying customers.

If you want to double your sales, you have several ways to do this. First, you can simply double the number of people entering this funnel—in other words, gain more traffic. This is why traffic-building strategies are so popular, and the tracking and numbers become so important, especially when you're spending money to bring more people into the funnel with ads and other paid tactics.

Here's the second option. Assuming the same amount of traffic, you can simply double the rate at which traffic converts to subscribers, or subscribers to clicks to a sales page, or sales page views to customers. It becomes a fun numbers game that involves testing new strategies that could have a massive impact on the bottom line.

Funnels are extremely important. By understanding a customer's journey, you're able to build a systematic operation that can actually make money for you, and that's the goal. You need to make money in order to stay in business and support your life, and understanding how customers enter the picture and complete the journey is vital to the success of any business.

Unfortunately in many cases, the funnels and the numbers behind them often become more important than the actual experiences that real human beings behind the numbers are having. Unless you're thinking hard about crafting your superfan journey—establishing all the moments within your brand that make people feel special—you're going to work really hard to get new people to enter your funnels, which can be exhausting and potentially very expensive.

I want you to be unexhausted and very much not bankrupt. Hence, I want to help you build your very own superfan army.

This book is all about defining what the superfan journey will look like for your business and brand—how the people who find you will become raving fans, will love and support you, and will share you and your work like their life depends on it. I'll be giving you several proven strategies that brands and businesses of all kinds have used to help their people climb this pyramid. It doesn't matter if you're a solo creator (like a YouTuber) or a huge company with thousands of employees (like YouTube itself)—this book will help you grow and activate your fanbase, and have fun doing it.

Maybe the best part about defining and creating your superfan journey? It's fun! Creating experiences that will move and inspire your audience to act and connect with you is exciting—way more fun than just number crunching and worrying about conversion rates and optimization. That stuff is important, of course. But if you're having more fun, you're going to be happier, and your business is going to thrive.

So get excited, because you're about to have a ton of fun creating your own unique superfan journey using the tactics, strategies, and stories in this book as your guide and inspiration.

Starting from the bottom of the pyramid, in **part 1**, I'll show you different ways you can convert casual audience members into active audience members. You'll learn some of the brilliant ways different brands, large and small, take their casual fans to the active stage, including how video game company Blizzard used one simple strategy to build a subscription-based business of over 5.5 million global subscribers. You'll also learn my Learn the Lyrics strategy, one I guarantee you've experienced before, except no one's pointed it out to you. I'll take you back to April's first trigger with the Backstreet Boys, the one that started it all, and why it wasn't that first time she heard them on the radio. And stick around for my special Drive the DeLorean strategy, which will help you take people from casual to active by painting them a detailed picture of their potential future.

In **part 2**, you'll continue up the pyramid and learn various ways you can captivate your active audience members and convert them into participants in a more engaged, connected community. You'll learn how to get your audience to speak up, participate, and feel invested in what you do. You'll see the strategies LEGO used to go from $800 million in debt and almost bankrupt to a company that's worth more than both Hasbro and Mattel combined—strategies you can use, no matter how big or small your brand may be. I'll also share a little American history lesson that will open up the doors for you and reveal possibilities for getting more people to talk about you and your brand as if they were a part of it themselves.

And in **part 3**, we'll cover how people in your connected community can turn into superfans. This is where we start to focus on creating those extra-special moments, ones that create novelty, defy expectations, and break the mold. These are the strategies that will help you make your fans feel like the heroes of their own story—the special access, unexpected one-on-one interactions, and one-of-a-kind experiences you'll deliver to create fans for life.

Each chapter focuses on a specific **strategy** for moving audience members into the next stage on the Pyramid of Fandom. I'll define the strategy and give you real-life examples of that strategy in action. At the end of each chapter, you'll see an **exercise** section. Each exercise will give you a way to execute on the strategy you've just learned so that you can actually put things into practice—and see results! I tried to make each exercise as easy as possible to grasp and implement, so that you'll be able to experience those results almost immediately. I also encourage you to share your results using the hashtag #SuperfansBook.

Throughout the entire journey, you'll learn powerful methods to create amazing, memorable, share-worthy experiences for your people. As you progress through the book and learn about each part of the pyramid, please understand that you do not need to do all of the things you're about to learn. Even a few of the strategies, when implemented, can create superfans for your brand. Pick and choose the ones that resonate with you and fit your style. The key is to understand the unique qualities and needs of each segment and tailor the ways you appeal to each one. Just the conscious effort alone will have you doing better than most of the competitors in your space.

Finally, **part 4** is where we cover the dark side of superfandom. These chapters are not meant to scare you, but rather to give you a glimpse of some of the dangers that can arise when you raise your profile and people become really invested in you. It's a big world, and you do need to play it safe.

Are you ready to begin building your very own superfan journey? Take a deep breath, because here we go!

PART 1

CASUAL AUDIENCE TO ACTIVE AUDIENCE

SUPERFANS

CONNECTED

ACTIVE

CASUAL

W e begin our journey at the base of the Pyramid of Fandom, which is the biggest segment: your casual audience members. These are the people who come to you randomly. They stumble upon your brand through a link on another website, or a Google or YouTube search, or maybe they found you through social media, or even by word of mouth. They're here because of their curiosity, but they may not stick around; they could take you or leave you. They might come back from time to time to see what you're up to, but they're not connected to your brand in a meaningful way—yet.

Your mission is to help bring these casual audience members, people who have just been introduced to you and what you have to offer, to the next level of the pyramid, where they become part of your active audience. Your active audience are your subscribers and followers. They're the ones who have subscribed to your emails, who now follow you on Facebook, Instagram, and YouTube. They're the people who have opted in—the ones who are interested in you and your brand, and have taken action to get more from it.

To move people from casual to active, you need to create a moment of activation—something that connects them to you and makes them go, "Oh, that's different, and I like it." You need to speak to people in a way they'll understand and appreciate, addressing their needs and pain points in the right language. And of course, you need to deliver them value! Give them a taste of what they'll get from you if they subscribe and stick around. Make it a no-brainer for them to take the next step and continue to hear from you.

These first five strategies are all about turning casual audience members into active participants in your brand:

- ▶ **CHAPTER 1: LEARN THE LYRICS**
- ▶ **CHAPTER 2: BREAK THE ICE**
- ▶ **CHAPTER 3: CREATE QUICK WINS**
- ▶ **CHAPTER 4: DRIVE THE DELOREAN**
- ▶ **CHAPTER 5: RETURN EVERY HANDSHAKE**

At this point, I'm sure you're wondering what the heck a DeLorean has to do with turning casual audience members into active ones. (You might even be wondering what the heck a DeLorean is ...)

But have no fear, as I'm about to explain it all ...

LEARN THE LYRICS

Before the whole "Box o' Backstreet Boys" incident went down, I'd been curious about exactly how April had become a superfan of the famous boy band. She told me a story that took us back to when she was only fifteen, just a couple years before I met her.

She had apparently gone through a pretty bad breakup with her boyfriend, the kind where you lock yourself in your room and blast the music really loud, which she did. Lying on her bed, a song popped up on the radio that she'd heard many times before, but this time, it was a much different experience.

She actually paid attention to what they were saying.

Why?

Because they were saying everything she was going through in that moment: the desire to turn back time, asking the person you love to stop playing games with your heart.

The song? You get half credit for guessing (because I basically gave it away): "Quit Playing Games (With My Heart)" by the Backstreet Boys.

That moment, combined with the song's message, was April's moment of activation. The lyrics grabbed her attention. They made her listen, and most importantly, they made her feel like the band knew what she was going through. Those lyrics had kick-started April's journey down the backstreets of superfandom.

The next time the hit song came on the radio, she would turn up the volume. When she had a chance to go to the store to buy their album, she did. She bought their posters and stuck them on her wall, watched their music videos after school on MTV's *Total Request Live* every day, and talked about them nonstop with her friends and family, so much so that her brother caved and bought her tickets to see the group in concert.

And it all started with getting the lyrics right.

Think about it. At the time, the target audience for the Backstreet Boys was teenage girls just like April. Their songs were about what many teenage girls think about and go through: love and heartbreak. And most importantly, the lyrics used the language of that audience; take a phrase like "Quit playing games with my heart," for example. A little kid doesn't say stuff like that, and adults are typically less melodramatic. Instead, it's a line aimed right at the teenage set. Those lyrics (and the band's many others) are precision crafted to get through to the band's ideal audience. It's a winning formula, one proven not just through record sales and platinum albums, but the fact that those teenage girls have now grown up and still sell out concert halls to watch BSB to this day. I know this because April went to see them recently.

Building a strong, successful brand is about solving people's problems. Step one is to know what those problems are, but step two, so often underrated and overlooked, is knowing exactly how those people describe their problems. The language they use should become the lyrics you use in your brand. Jay Abraham, a businessman and author responsible for developing a lot of direct response marketing strategies in the 1970s that we still use today, once said, "If you can define the problem better than your target customer, they will automatically assume you have the solution." When a potential customer hears you speak about exactly what they are going through, in a way that they can relate, they're going to say to themselves, "They get me. They understand." And that's a powerful trigger to set yourself apart from the many others who are fighting for this potential customer's attention. Sing the right lyrics, and you're going to get people to stick with you. You're going to activate them.

If you're trying to build an audience of superfans, what are your lyrics? They're the words you use to communicate with that audience: the ones in your emails, blog articles, videos, Facebook posts, your keynote addresses, and even the casual conversations you have with people you meet at events or on the street. Using the right lyrics is a powerful signal to your audience that you care about them enough to "speak their language."

In my own business, speaking the language of my target audience is incredibly important. I always pay careful attention to the language people use in their emails, on Facebook and Instagram, and in person, so that I can use that language myself. Once in a while, I even reach out to ten people on my email list to have an open conversation about what they're dealing with in their own business and how I could better serve them. Paying attention to what my customers are saying in these different ways gives me incredibly valuable information about what they need, and how they describe those needs—as well as what they *don't* need. Then, of course, that information needs to be put into action. There are a lot of ways you can learn the language of your audience. Here are three ways you can do this right now.

Method 1: Find conversations that are already happening online.

People are talking online, right now, about their pains and problems—some of which relate to the solutions you're creating for them. These conversations are happening on social media and blogs, and in groups and forums, and with a little bit of effort, you can find them and learn from them.

Finding existing conversations online can be a valuable exercise that reveals a lot about your target audience (i.e. the people who are attracted to you and the way you do things) and how they describe what they're going through. That said, this isn't the best strategy because you aren't having direct conversations with that audience. But if you're just starting out and have no contacts, no audience, no email list, and no relationships with anyone in the space you're going into, method 1 is a good place to begin.

GROUPS ON FACEBOOK OR LINKEDIN

Groups on social media channels like Facebook or LinkedIn are amazing tools for conducting research and finding conversations. In the search bar at the top, type in some keywords that you believe your target audience may be using to find each other. For example, if you're in the homeschooling niche, obviously you'd type in "homeschooling" or "homeschool." A number of groups (among other results, like pages or people) will appear. Filter out everything but the groups, if possible.

You may have to be a little creative in the keywords you use. Also, think outside your niche. For example, one level beyond "homeschooling" might be something like "education" or "parenting." I can imagine some interesting discussions related to the pros and cons of homeschooling in groups related to either of those categories, too.

On Facebook, some of these groups are public, which you do not need to join in order to see the discussions. Other groups are closed, which require an admin to approve you first before seeing any of the discussions inside. DO NOT (I repeat: DO NOT) go into these groups to spam your business or share your latest creations. This turns people off, and you're likely to be banned quickly. Your role, instead, is to find out what people are talking about, and more importantly, *how* they're talking about it.

Now, there are going to be a lot of discussions, especially in the more active groups. There'll be some spam (don't do it!), random conversations, and lots of questions. To help you narrow down your search for useful discussions, use this quick trick.

In the search bar within the group, usually located in the sidebar, type in the following phrases to help you find the goods. Make sure to include quotation marks to get exact matches:

- ► "why is it"
- ► "when can I"
- ► "what are the"
- ► "what is the"

- ▶ "how come I"
- ▶ "need help"
- ▶ "please help"
- ▶ "I need"
- ▶ "help with"

What's great is that this method can also be used in forums, blogs and even on Google! You can learn more about this approach in my book *Will It Fly?*.

Again, this method is a good start, but I want to share two even better ways to find out what people need help with by having actual conversations with them.

Method 2: Describe your biggest challenge related to _____.

This method is something I learned from Ryan Levesque, who wrote the book *Ask: The Counterintuitive Online Method to Discover Exactly What Your Customers Want to Buy … Create a Mass of Raving Fans … and Take Any Business to the Next Level.* Simply ask people about their biggest challenge related to a specific topic, then follow up with them to learn more. If your business involves helping people succeed with their podcasts, maybe it's asking about the biggest challenges they encounter when finding interview guests for their show. Then, reach out via email or direct message to the people who respond to ask follow-up questions. I think you'll find people are more than happy to share a lot of valuable details that will help you create and refine products and services to address their pain points.

Although one of my favorite ways to do this is by reaching out to people on my email list, you can definitely use this strategy if you don't have a big following of active subscribers yet. Simply make your question one of the first things people see when they come across your brand even if they haven't yet subscribed to your email list or followed you on social media. Post your question on social media where even a casual visitor will see it and have a chance to respond.

As you grow your active audience, you can continue to take advantage of this strategy. I started using it in 2014, and it was game-changing. I sent an email out that included an open-ended survey question: What's your number one challenge related to building an online business? I received more than 7,000 responses, and I used those lyrics to inform the language in my sales copy, emails, and much more.

That exercise also helped us determine that there were three different groups of people in my audience: people who didn't have a business yet, people who'd started but hadn't seen significant results, and people who'd started and achieved good results. This led us to create three separate audience buckets that we talk to in different ways on the website and through email, and influences the products and services we create for them.

Even if you don't have a huge audience, you can still take advantage of asking open-ended questions like this. For example, you could include a similar question in an email in the autoresponder series people receive after they subscribe to your list. You'll get a continuous stream of answers as people join, and you can then follow up with them.

When you follow up, ask questions like, *What kinds of solutions have you tried so far? If you had a magic wand to solve this challenge, what would things look like for you?* I promise you'll receive a ton of incredibly valuable information you'll be able to feed directly back into your business.

Method 3: Real-Life Conversations

These days, a simple face-to-face conversation can seem almost . . . revolutionary. This one is simple, and is similar to method 2: Find ten people, and ask them to spend fifteen minutes talking to you about a problem or need they have related to your area of expertise or interest.

Even after growing my own email list to 200,000 people, I still make an effort to have conversations with at least ten new subscribers every single month. I'll pick ten random people from my email list and send them a quick note asking if they'll hop on a video call with me for fifteen minutes to talk about what they're going through and how I can help. It is essential for me to stay connected to who the people in my audience are, how I can help them, and the language they use.

When you're just starting out, you may not have many fans or email list subscribers, but that's okay. The beauty of this method is that it's doable even before you have an email list or many followers. Find people at events like conventions or meetups, or online in Facebook or LinkedIn groups. Invite them to talk to you on a conference call, on the phone, or in person!

One conversation can reveal a lot! When you speak directly with someone, you not only hear their words, but you also feel the emotion that comes along with them, something that's often lost in the online space. That emotional element allows you to connect more deeply with people and better understand them, which will help you create better content, products, and services for them.

Once you've found the people in your target audience and begun learning about their problems—and most importantly, how they talk about those problems—you'll be setting yourself up to connect with that audience authentically and effectively for as long as you're in business. Now that you understand the importance of getting the lyrics down, in the next chapter I'll tell you why you need to start thinking about the "singer" (that's you), and how you can add your own story, personality, and interests to those lyrics so you can stand out from the crowd even more.

EXERCISE

Learn the language your audience uses—especially how they describe their pains, problems, and needs—and put it into action.

STEP 1

Choose at least one of the methods above and find five key phrases that your audience uses to describe their problems/what they're going through. You'll probably find it helpful to try two at minimum: method 1 in combination with either method 2 or 3.

STEP 2

Once you have your five key phrases, practice writing something, whether it's an email, social media post, or blog article, incorporating the language you identified in step 1 and send it or post it to test the response you get from your audience.

LET'S GO DEEPER

I recorded a quick video to demonstrate this exercise for you, and I've also created a helpful spreadsheet you can use to track your findings. They're in chapter 1 of your bonus *Superfans* Bonus Companion Course, which you can get access to at **yoursuperfans.com/course**.

CHAPTER 02

BREAK
THE ICE

B ack in 2010 I attended my first conference: Blog World Expo, in
Las Vegas, Nevada. I had been blogging from home for about two
years and felt it was the right time to venture out into the real world and
meet other people in person—despite the fact that the introvert in me
was having doubts. I was comfortable with the setup I had at home: communication via a keyboard with no face-to-face interactions required.
However, I understood the potential value that could come from a trip
like this, so I bought a ticket to the event and drove six hours from San
Diego to Las Vegas the day before the event.

On the drive, as I typically do before trying something new, I began
to have doubts. I wasn't 100 percent sure how useful this event was going
to be for me, but beyond questioning the subject matter of the presentations, would I even connect with anyone new while there? I knew there
would be a lot of people (several thousand), but would I actually find
people in the crowd that I'd want to continue a relationship with? How
would I even do that?

The next morning, as the keynote presentation was about to get un-
derway, I sat in a random row surrounded by people I didn't know apart

from the first name on their name tag. I felt too scared to initiate a conversation. Thankfully, the guy sitting to my right reached out to shake my hand.

"Hi, Pat. I'm Dave. So what's your blog about?"

Honestly, I don't even remember if this person's name was actually Dave, because after a quick introduction, everyone one else around us started to stand and introduce themselves, too. There was a Jim (probably not a Jim), a Dana (probably not a Dana), and a Richard (also probably not a Richard).

And each time, it was the exact same conversation:

"Hi, nice to meet you. This is my blog. I'm from here. Have you been to this conference before?"

Then behind me, I met Harris. Harris's name is actually Harris. I remember Harris because this is how the conversation went:

"Hi, Pat. I'm Harris. I left my wife at home with my kids to be here. How about you?"

It was an odd start, I'll admit, but what was more interesting was my response:

"Hey, Harris. Nice to meet you. Funny, my wife is here with a one-year-old, and I left her in the hotel room."

That was the moment the ice was broken. And by *ice* I mean the cold introductions we'd made earlier. We had a quick conversation about what blogging was like with kids in the house, since he had a five-year-old and a two-year-old. I began to ask questions about the two-year-old since he was very close in age to my son and I was still in the "I have no idea what to expect as a new parent" phase.

The keynote eventually started, and we took our seats. I have no recollection of who was on stage or what the keynote was about, but after the presentation Harris and I decided to continue our conversation over lunch, when I found out about his tech blog and the fun plans he had for it. He doesn't blog anymore, but we're still friends and keep in touch on social media to this day.

So what happened here? How were Harris and I able to strike up a relationship when I'd already been introduced and talked with several others right before him? It wasn't his firm handshake or the fancy business card he'd printed. And it wasn't the fact that he started off the conversation in a funny way. We gravitated toward each other because we had something in common that we could talk about together: kids.

When an engaged couple plans the seating arrangement at their wedding reception, is it a completely random selection? No way! It's a careful puzzle that's constructed so that everyone is seated next to people they can relate to. The friends from high school all have their own table. The college tennis team sits together (in the back, because they can get a little rowdy sometimes). And the tweens and teens are all at a table together. When you're with someone you can relate to and have something in common with, you're more likely to have a good time.

When it comes to your brand and business, you're having conversations with new people you've never met before all of the time. They come across your videos, listen to your podcasts, read your blogs, or see your tweets and posts, and if the content answers their questions and is valuable, they might even begin to follow your work. But when you add personality into the mix and inject elements that your audience can relate to, then they're not just going to follow your work. They're going to follow *you*.

This is how you start to develop a true rapport with your audience and turn casual visitors into active followers. When you introduce points of connection, it gives people an opportunity to say, "Hey I like that thing too!" *and* it connects you with that thing in their mind. They're going to link you with something they love. It's an *association of appreciation*.

To create that association, you need to start doing what I like to call *breaking the ice* in your business: Get comfortable sharing things about yourself and your life, perhaps outside of the realm of your niche but also more personal, in order to bring attention to the person behind the brand and foster meaningful connections with your audience. As one of my best friends, Chris Ducker from Youpreneur.com, says, "It's not about B to B or B to C. It's about P to P: the person-to-person relationship." People choose to work with and invest in other people, and if you're not doing that, your business isn't going to reach its potential. Period.

Fun fact: Chris and I met at that same event in 2010 where I met Harris. I had hired his company, VirtualStaffFinder.com, to find a virtual assistant for my business prior to the event, and during a lunch meeting we had, we both found out we were married to Filipina women and each had a boy around the same age! We immediately bonded and hung out the rest of the conference, and to this day, Chris and I are like brothers. A much older brother (joking, lol), but one of the cool ones you always want to hang out with.

So, back to breaking the ice. What's the trick here? *How* do you actually implement this? It's quite easy: Share stuff about yourself that you'd share with your friends. Say you're reading a good book; is it worth sharing with your friends? Maybe. If that's something you'd do, then share it with your audience! Maybe you're enjoying a great breakfast from Roscoe's Chicken and Waffles; is that worth sharing with your friends? Maybe. If you'd normally do that, then do it! If not, then don't. If you're watching a basketball game and you're thrilled that your home team won the championship, would you share that experience with your friends? Maybe. Share that, too!

You don't have to share every waking moment of your life, because guess what? Your friends don't necessarily want to hear about every waking moment of your life. But there's still a lot you can and should share if you want people to get a sense of who you are as a person behind the brand.

You can share these kinds of things any way you're comfortable. Maybe it's on social media, or in your YouTube videos. Adding a personal touch to your presentations is a great way to make a noteworthy first impression.

One of my favorite ways to break the ice is to inject some personality into things I'm already doing and teaching. For example, if you were teaching personal development in a blog post, instead of "10 Things You Should Know About Personal Development," make that blog post "10 Things Harry Potter Can Teach You About Personal Development," and use your love for Harry Potter to make things more interesting. Will everyone in your audience love Harry Potter? No. Some will, and they'll immediately gravitate toward you and get excited to learn more from you. But for the others, will they go away? Not usually! You don't break up with your friends when they're a fan of something that you're not a fan of, right? So there's really nothing to lose here! As long as you continue to add value, you can add your personality and make a ton of connections with a lot of new people without sounding "just like the other guys."

Want some real-life examples of this? Here are a few.

Video software company Wistia isn't afraid to tell you all about Lenny. Who's Lenny? Lenny is a forty-five-pound red labradoodle who's also the company's unofficial mascot. He even attends company meetings. In 2016, Wistia went so far as to launch "StartPup: A Competition for Startups with Dogs" to break the ice with people at other startups around the world who share a love for our furry friends. It's pretty clear: The people of Wistia love dogs, and they're not afraid to share it—because they know people in their audience who love dogs are going to love them even more for it!

On a more serious note, one of the people I most admire in the online business space is Chalene Johnson, who's an incredible entrepreneur in the physical fitness space. In a Facebook video a couple of years ago, she opened up about her struggles with her own marriage. It was an incredibly vulnerable thing to do, but rather than turn people off, many in her audience applauded and thanked her for her raw honesty and vulnerability. Chalene showed how powerful it can be to be truly human and vulnerable, even if you have a business with a huge audience.

Breaking the ice can also be as simple as inviting your audience in and creating a space for them to share and connect with others. For four years, social media company Buffer used their weekly "Buffer Chat" (hashtagged as #bufferchat) to allow for one-to-many communication between the brand and its community. As the company's official blog put it in 2016, #bufferchat was designed as "a place for our community to come together, meet each other, and learn from each other." Buffer retired the chat in 2018, but it was incredibly successful, with many chats drawing more than 400 participants.

Remember, what you put out you're going to attract. However you choose to break the ice, it needs to be authentic. If you pretend to be like something or someone else, you're not only going to risk being called out, but you'll also attract the kinds of people you might not want to attract. For example, if you pretend to be rich and famous by posting images on Instagram of really nice cars and mansions that you just rented (but you "forgot" to mention that point), you might attract a large audience of people who are fascinated by all things "bling," but chances are they're only going to follow you because you're sharing nice cars and things they wish they had too, instead of being attracted to you for who you really are.

In 2010, before my podcast went live, I had an idea to hopefully inject some humanity into my show and make some real connections with people. At the beginning of each of my podcast episodes, I'd have my voiceover guy read a fun ten-second fact about me in the intro. Every single time. I shared this idea with a number of friends and colleagues who were already podcasting, and here was the general consensus:

"Pat, that's one of the dumbest ideas I've ever heard. Why would you waste people's time, and even waste your own money having your voice-over guy do that? Listeners just want to get to the content they came for."

Now, I do listen to my friends and mentors, and much of my business journey has been shaped by them and their feedback. But sometimes you just need to follow your gut, and this was one of those moments. I decided to give it a shot and see what would happen. And now, more than fifty million downloads later, many of these same people who told me not to do it are now telling me:

"Pat, you're a genius."

I'm not a genius, though. I just know that people want to feel like they have a friend—and what do friends know about each other sometimes? Random facts that the person will feel special about knowing. Now, when I go to conferences, I have fans come up to me and start talking like we've been friends for years. I have to remember to ask for their name sometimes because we're often already deep into conversation about something before I've even had a chance to ask.

If anyone who has listened to my show has ever been in a marching band, we can instantly turn into band nerds and start sharing stories from the good ol' days. I've mentioned that I'm half-Filipino before, and whenever I meet another Filipino person, it's the first thing they bring up. I even once had a person call me a "big baby" the first time they met me—not because I'm a big baby (although maybe you could argue that sometimes), but because I'd mentioned in one of my episodes that I was born 11 lbs. 12 oz., and the person who said this to me had given birth to a big baby. She could relate. (By the way, you can subscribe to both my podcasts at yoursuperfans.com/spipodcast.)

But perhaps the biggest thing I've become known for outside of my business because of this strategy is the deep tie between Pat Flynn and the greatest movie of all time, *Back to the Future*. The real me is someone who absolutely loves—like seriously—this movie. And if I've been able to help people, a common way they thank me is by sending me a package with a *Back to the Future* gift. Here's a picture of many of the things people have sent me. (I did not buy any of this.)

I don't share this to show off or share how wonderful my fans are (though they are the best!), but rather that people gravitate toward what they begin to know about you. Sure, not everyone is a *BTTF* fan, but they know it's something I like and my fandom is the kind of thing you'd learn about a friend.

Naturally, I love to inject my *BTTF* fascination into my content, particularly the talks I give at big conferences. Keynote presentations are an especially great way to put yourself into your message, because you're speaking live to a captive audience. In 2015, I gave the keynote address at New Media Expo (NMX) in Las Vegas. You could say I went all out. Before I came onstage, the audience watched a short film I created that had a *Back to the Future* theme. I arrived onstage in—you might have guessed it—a DeLorean, the iconic time-traveling car from the *BTTF* movies. As for the presentation itself, it was all about how to futureproof your brand, and the *Back to the Future* theme was my way of aligning with that theme while also injecting a lot of my personality into it. It was also the thirty-year anniversary of the first *Back to the Future* movie that year, which made the event extra special.

(Yes, I know I said you shouldn't try to attract people using cars, but this is the exception that proves the rule.)

Since then, people in my audience now associate me with *Back to the Future*. Check it out:

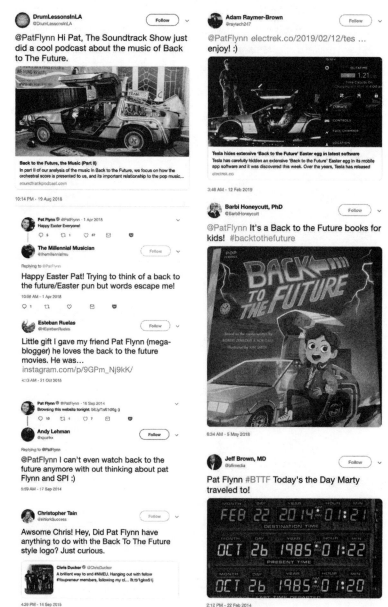

Pretty wild, huh? And now, because of this, every time *Back to the Future* is mentioned in the news, or someone in my audience spots a DeLorean randomly on the road, they're thinking about me, just like you will now, too. See how that works? It's powerful stuff, and it's just about being more human.

You've learned the lyrics and broken the ice, so it's time to get down to business and give people what they came for: some serious value, delivered with as little fuss as possible. You're about to learn about the two-pronged power of the small, quick win, and how you can use it to turn one-time visitors into regulars.

EXERCISE

Share something about yourself with your audience in a way you haven't done before.

STEP 1

Share something as simple as a small post on your favorite social media channel, or just a couple of seconds in a podcast or video you publish. It doesn't have to be huge or overly produced.

STEP 2

Use your own voice, and don't go beyond what you're not comfortable sharing. You might just find groups of people in your audience who can totally relate!

STEP 3

Last thing: Don't try to measure the results. This isn't a ploy to collect likes or new subscribers. This is simply a way for you to share more about yourself, and become more human to your audience as a result.

LET'S GO DEEPER

I have a lot more examples of breaking the ice that may inspire you for this exercise. Make sure to check them out in chapter 2 of your *Superfans* Bonus Companion Course, which you can get access to at **yoursuperfans.com/course**.

CHAPTER 03

CREATE QUICK WINS

Before I started my business, I was a huge personal finance nerd. Every paycheck I received from my architecture job was carefully deconstructed, and I knew exactly where all of it was going, down to the penny. My 401(k) was growing steadily, and it was normal for me to spend some time every week calculating the growth trajectory of my accounts forty years down the road. Age sixty-five, here I come!

I subscribed to a number of blogs about personal finance, always looking for the best long-term strategies for income growth and investments. There are thousands of them, and I had a few of my favorites in my morning reading agenda: GetRichSlowly.org, SimpleDollar.com, and ManvsDebt.com were just a few of the dozens I followed eagerly.

During a lunch break at work one day, I came across an edgier blog in the personal finance space called *I Will Teach You to Be Rich,* authored by Ramit Sethi. I'd heard about him and his blog, but had stayed away because the name was off-putting to me. You'll teach me to be rich—really? I'd read all the strategies about long-term, safe investments—or so I thought.

I clicked on a link from another website to one of Ramit's new articles about how to save thousands of dollars in ten minutes with one simple phone call. It seemed too good to be true, but ten minutes? I could spare ten minutes to see if it would work. Here's what Ramit suggested in his article:

1. Call your cable company.
2. Read his script to negotiate a lower monthly payment.
3. Enjoy the extra $.

During lunch, I called my cable company, followed the script, and guess what? It worked! I was able to save 20 percent per month on my bill in just ten minutes. I was hooked. Ramit became my favorite blogger. I went back into his archive and read every single post. I downloaded his ebook. And later, I eventually paid for his products. All because he'd hooked me in with a small, quick win. And that's the trick:

Give your audience a small, quick win.

Charles Duhigg, author of *The Power of Habit*, dedicates an entire chapter to the power of the small, quick win. As he states, "Small wins fuel transformative changes by leveraging tiny advantages into patterns that convince people that bigger achievements are within reach."

In the book *Atomic Habits*, James Clear gives an example of the small, quick win in action in your own life. If you want to start building a habit of running every day, set out your next morning's running clothes the night before. That way, when you wake up, you don't even have to think about finding them, so you'll be more likely to do your workout.

We all want to do as much as we can for the people in our audience, but if you want to change their lives, start by changing their day first. That small, quick win could convert a brand new visitor into a returning subscriber, customer, and fan.

Here are some amazing examples of how companies are using small, quick wins to create big results:

Blizzard, the game company behind the popular worldwide multi-player game *World of Warcraft* sucked in millions of people, including me, by making the first five minutes of the game incredibly rewarding. After selecting your character and getting dropped into the game, after you slay a few creatures and find a few treasures, you're bumped up to experience level two, which means you unlock new abilities *and* get motivated to move up to level three, where even more goodies will be available. I actually had to delete the game from my computer my third year of college because I was staying up for forty-eight hours straight at times just to get to the next level. It was pretty sad saying goodbye to my level sixty mage.

I don't blame Blizzard for using quick wins to make their game more addictive. Of course they'd want to keep people playing. But you can still take advantage of the Blizzard-style small, quick win to build your own superfan army without causing them to subsist entirely on Cheetos and Mountain Dew and forget what day it is.

Then there's Walid Azami from HowtoPhotograph.net, who I had on the *AskPat* podcast in 2018. Walid was (and still is!) a successful photographer with an amazing portfolio of clients. (Think Mariah Carey, Madonna, Kanye West . . .) But he was unhappy with how people in his industry went out of their way to *not* help each other, and he vowed to go about things differently. So he secretly started an Instagram account called @HowtoPhotograph. As Walid says, "I just put myself out there with zero followers, and I started helping photographers little nugget by little nugget with lighting tips, composition tips, business advice, how to talk to a customer, how to negotiate, how to get out of a heated situation." Gradually, he built up a huge following, mainly thanks to his generosity and the small, quick wins he helped his fellow photographers achieve every day.

Finally, many companies use the small, quick win to put people's fears at ease and get them excited to face a challenge as part of their new-user-onboarding process. Codecademy, which provides a range of courses to help people learn programming and other technical skills, does this by making a complex skill that takes a long time to master—coding—a lot more approachable. When you sign up as a new user, you get an email inviting you to try out a fun mini coding project, one in which you create an interactive animated version of your name using the Java-Script language in just thirty minutes. It's fun, and it quickly gives you a sense of progress toward your goal of becoming a coding master.

And we're still barely scratching the surface of what's possible with the small, quick win! Here are a few more ideas I've used to create small, quick wins in my own business that you can capitalize on, too.

Give People a Challenge

My "100 Email" challenge, which you can find at 100emails.com, is one way I give people a small, quick win by getting their first hundred email subscribers. Why one hundred? Because it's much more doable than something like 100,000. With the right approach, you could get to one hundred subscribers in just a few days, which is exactly how the challenge works—it's a seventy-two-hour "email list ultimatum" that walks you step-by-step through the process of getting from zero to one hundred subscribers. And it's designed to help people start accruing small wins as quickly as possible. Just getting to their first ten subscribers helps people think, "Yes, I can do this! I can keep going." Even landing one additional subscriber when your list is still really small can be super exciting! And the "challenge" aspect, along with the three-day time limit, is like a bow on top, creating suspense and excitement that makes it even more rewarding when people score that win and reach their goal.

Load Your First Email with Small, Quick Win Potential

When you have an email list, it's a great idea to make sure the first email people get from you is full of value and delivers a quick win—ideally something they can do in less than five minutes. A small, quick win method I used for a long time in my first email that used to work really well (though I've since changed it) was a tip to help content creators figure out what they should be talking about on their blog, podcast, or YouTube channel—a topic-inspiration quick win.

The method involves going to Amazon, looking up books related to your topic, then using the free preview to examine the table of contents. You're not copying the table of contents, but using it as inspiration for the kinds of content you should be creating and sharing with your audience. For example, if you were to look up a fly fishing book and peek inside, you might see a chapter related to tying knots. That might inspire you to write a blog post on the top three ways to tie a fly in less than ten minutes. You'll know that post will be relevant because it was inspired by something important enough to be its own section in a published book on the same topic.

As a result of sharing this win, I had loads of people reply to that email saying thank you and it was just the thing they needed to help them with ideas for their content. A number of them even wrote that they were already excited about reading the next email!

Pack Your Getting Started Page with Small, Quick Wins

When you're helping people do something—learn a skill, build a business, etc.—give them a one-stop shop to get started with that thing and build up some small, quick wins. A great way to do this is through a "getting started" page on your website. For example, let's say your business involves helping people podcast. You can deliver a number of quick wins from that one page by packing it with resources and information about what gear to purchase, how to find guests for their show, and how to figure out what the first few episodes will be about. Finding all this great info will almost be a quick win of its own for your readers, one that will motivate them to continue on their new journey knowing that there's so much content available in one place to support them.

The small, quick win is like a 5-Hour Energy shot for your audience, one that'll jump-start their journey to superfandom by motivating them to want to keep hearing from you (minus the caffeine jitters!). In the next chapter, I'll let you in on the incredible power of storytelling, and how you can paint a picture of two possible futures to inspire your casual audience to take action with you. The best part: this next strategy gives me an excuse to talk about *Back to the Future* again.

EXERCISE

Find opportunities to give your audience quick wins and get them psyched to keep hearing from you.

STEP 1

Audit all the places in your brand where your audience first hears from you. First, identify the different ways and places people hear from you after initiating their relationship with you—the first email they receive or the getting started page on your website is a good place to start.

STEP 2

Ask, does what I share in this email or on this page provide the person with a quick win . . . or am I just hitting them with more information?

STEP 3

Brainstorm ways you could transform the content of that page or email to give the person a small, quick win. And if that email or page already contains guidance on getting a quick win, how could you make that win more impactful or quicker to achieve (or both)?

LET'S GO DEEPER

For more examples of how I use quick wins in my brand to create an initial *wow* moment for my fans—for inspiration (and literally just to copy them!)—check out chapter 3 in the *Superfans* Bonus Companion Course at **yoursuperfans.com/course.**

DRIVE THE DELOREAN

I t was the summer of 2012. Shane Sams was at home in Kentucky, in his front yard, mowing his lawn on his riding lawn mower. He usually listened to music to pass the time, but that day he wanted something a little different. Scrolling through Apple Podcasts, he stumbled across my podcast and hit play.

Shane was mowing along, listening to the show, when something he heard piqued his interest. He leapt off the lawn mower and ran toward the house. As he burst into the kitchen, his wife, Jocelyn, was there with their kids, Isaac and Anna.

"Jocelyn, you've got to listen to this! This is our destiny! We're going to change our lives!" Shane was fired up and breathless. "This guy Pat Flynn is talking about making money online and passive income. I don't even know what that means, but it sounds great! Let's do it!"

"What?" came Jocelyn's reply. "How are you going to do that? The people who do that are not normal people. They're probably just lucky or something." Inspired but deflated, Shane headed back outside to finish cutting the grass.

But that wasn't the end of Shane and Jocelyn's story. In fact, it was just the beginning.

Time machines haven't been invented (yet), but it's super fun to imagine if they had been. That's why I'm a superfan of the movie *Back to the Future*. Sure, the story is great and the characters are fun, but it's the idea of traveling through time that fascinates me the most. Bonus points for the DeLorean, of course.

You can also use time travel to take people from casual to active on the Pyramid of Fandom. Wondering how things are going to turn out in the future is something that's on every person's mind, and the more you can paint a picture of what a person's life could be like if they take action with you, the more likely they are to do that and become a fan.

There are two aspects to this strategy: painting a picture of the future of what life will be like if they **DO** take action with you, and what life will be like if they **DON'T**. You're going to help your audience "time travel" to two potential futures by telling a story of what life could be like if they don't make a change, then on the flipside, showing what's possible by sharing stories of people who were in their exact position not too long ago and turned things around with your help.

Let's start with the **DON'T** part of the strategy—painting a picture of life without your help. To craft that not-so-rosy picture, the very first thing you have to do is identify the problem you are solving for that person. You're not judging, but identifying their experience as it currently is and helping that person become even more aware of it.

And to do that effectively, you have to amplify the problem. Amplification is essentially making it very clear to someone what will happen if they don't take action. This might be describing what someone could negatively experience if they don't launch their podcast—all the lost potential they'll be giving up and the regret they'll feel about not following through on their vision. Or if you're helping people with weight loss, this could involve painting a picture of a heavy person's future, such as not being able to keep up with the kids, diabetes, heart issues, money spent on health bills, etc. The key is to provide lots of detail—again, you're painting a picture, not just drawing a sketch.

Focusing on a potentially negative future picture will capture the attention of a percentage of people in your audience and motivate them to take action. The key is to be sure you know exactly what your audience is afraid of, what keeps them up at night. This is where "learning the right lyrics" and understanding your audience's problems and desires, in their language, is crucial. But there's something really important to keep in mind here. When you give people a potential image of their future without your help, you have to be careful to not prey on their fears. There's a fine line between amplifying a problem and using fear and shame to bring someone around to your side. Use your power wisely and compassionately.

So we've addressed the **DON'T** side—what a target audience member's future might look like without your help. And while this will motivate some people to take action, you're going to be even more successful when you provide a counterpoint to that gloomy picture—which brings us to the **DO** side.

Once you've made the problem super clear, and showed someone their possible future if they don't deal with that issue, you need to tell them a **story** of what their problem looks like once it's been **solved**. It could be the story of how you solved it for yourself, or it could be the story of how you helped a client or customer find the solution on their own.

You see, your audience won't be buying your product or service— they'll be buying the change that product or service offers them. They'll be buying the way it will help them transform their lives. They'll be buying the solution, and you need to tell them a compelling story about how that solution works.

How do you do that? You need to show them examples of **transformation**—your solution in action. You need to give people a chance to see the change as it happens, in the lives of actual people. You need to paint a picture of how your solution can create direct positive change for someone.

Here is where your past experience with your audience—your clients or customers—will come in very handy. One of the best ways to paint that picture of transformation is by using **testimonials**. It's one thing to tell people what will happen if they follow you or use your product, but it's another to *prove* that your stuff works by showing people who were just like them not too long ago and how well they are doing now. Testimonials are incredibly powerful—and often a lot less work than trying to tell the transformation story yourself!

Which brings me back to Shane and Jocelyn Sams.

Shane kept listening to the *SPI Podcast* that day on the lawn mower in 2012—and for many days after, eventually getting through every episode in the archive. Over the course of the following two years, he and Jocelyn used what they'd learned from SPI to turn themselves into two of the "lucky" people. They each started out teaching what they know online: Shane taught football coaches new plays, and Jocelyn was helping librarians. In the years since that first fateful mower ride, they've started their own podcast and built an incredible online business called Flipped Lifestyle that has allowed them to quit their jobs and helps thousands of others build businesses of their own.

So what does this all have to do with time travel, DeLoreans, and DOs and DON'Ts? Well, Shane and Jocelyn were the featured guests on *SPI Podcast* episode 122 back in 2014. In that episode, they told the story of their online business-building journey, starting with that day in the backyard in Kentucky. Their success has been so massive that I even had them back a few years later, on *SPI Podcast* episode 265.

But that first episode is a special one because it's a phenomenal example of two people who followed someone's advice—who chose the path of DO—and made it work for them in a big way. In fact, it's become one of the most shared episodes of my podcast—even more than episodes featuring famous people like Tim Ferriss and Gary Vaynerchuk, who have shared plenty of amazing, inspiring stories of their own. Why? Because Shane and Jocelyn, a football coach and a librarian respectively, two "regular" folks from Kentucky, are probably a little more relatable to most people in my audience than icons like Tim or Gary (as awesome as they are). And so their testimony carries a little more weight. When people hear the Sams' story, they can hear themselves saying the same things. They feel like they know Shane and Jocelyn, because Shane and Jocelyn were just like them, not very long ago.

Whether it's in a DeLorean or on a riding mower, if you want to activate your casual audience, you need to take them on a preview journey of their possible futures—both with your help and without it. In the next and final strategy of part 1, I'll tell you why the simple act of shaking someone's hand can flip the switch for someone who's on the fence about your brand.

EXERCISE

Collect stories of positive transformation from your audience.

STEP 1

Gather at least five stories that show how what you teach or provide can help change people's lives or businesses (or both!) for the better. Ask people to give you the **before** (what their life was like before they learned from you or worked with you), the **after** (what their life was like after doing so), and the **what if** (what life would be like if they hadn't followed your advice).

STEP 2

Incorporate these stories into the messages you share with your audience. Think of five specific ways you can share these stories, whether that's in a blog article or in a podcast episode like I did with the Sams. If you want to see this in action even sooner (so *you* can achieve your own quick win), publish a detailed post on Facebook or Instagram highlighting one of these stories, and make sure you make it about them—not you.

RETURN EVERY HANDSHAKE

I was about to give the keynote address at a conference a few years ago. As I made my way to the stage, I tripped and fell on the stairs. But it was no accident. Instead of dusting myself off and continuing up to the stage, I "rewound" my fall, retracing my steps in reverse, then pausing and repeating my approach with zero mishaps. I made it all the way up to the stage, no worse for the wear and excited to deliver my keynote.

The point I was trying to make with my little stunt was this—and although it may sound cliché, it's true—in business, you only get one chance to make a first impression. And in a similar way, when it comes to the people in your casual audience who are finding you for the first time, you may only get one chance to connect with and welcome them in before they leave your brand for better pastures.

It's one thing to stumble when someone says hello to you and your brand. But it's another thing entirely to not even attempt to return the greeting.

Think of the handshake. A simple gesture, but one that's recognized across countries and cultures. The handshake may be the closest thing humans have to a universal greeting. Now imagine you're about to meet someone for the first time. You walk up to them, reach out your hand,

and . . . nothing. The other person just stands there, hands in their pockets, looking at you blankly. How would you feel?

Now pretend that instead of offering a physical handshake, a person comes to your Facebook page and asks a question on one of your posts. Their question sits quietly for a few days, getting no attention from you. Now you're the person on the other side of the (so far one-sided) interaction. Eventually, that person shrugs and gives up on you. It's just one missed connection, but it's also one lost potential superfan.

Don't leave anyone hanging. Follow up with everybody, especially when it's their first interaction with your brand. That first extended handshake from a person who's coming across you for the first time can be nothing short of a do-or-die moment for you in terms of whether you're going to form a vibrant superfan relationship with them—or if they're going to walk away with a bitter taste in their mouth and the urge to say unflattering things about you whenever they get the opportunity.

Unfortunately, every day online there are virtual handshakes left unmet. In my early days of online business, I thrived on returning every handshake—responding to every email, Facebook comment, tweet, you name it. I wanted everyone to know that I appreciated them, whether they'd been with me for years or had just stumbled across me earlier that day. But as my brand got bigger and I got busier, it got harder and harder to do that. At one point, my email inbox hovered around ten thousand unread messages. Each new email that arrived became a constant reminder of just how many people I wasn't able to answer, and it made me think about who I was letting down. It's hard to say how many potential superfans were lost to the ether because of my inability to respond to all those messages.

Thankfully, I recognized that I needed to create a system to help me respond to people. In 2014, I hired my assistant, Jess, to help manage my inbox. Together, we came up with a system to tackle the bloat, and with Jess leading the charge, we got it back to inbox zero.[2] (I don't think there's any magic to inbox zero, by the way—but it sure beats inbox ten thousand!) Since then, Jess has become my executive assistant, helping

---

[2] You can hear how we did this in *SPI Podcast* episode 115, found at https://www.smartpassiveincome.com/podcasts/email-management/

me keep the whole business organized and ensuring we respond to everyone who contacts us. She never pretends to be me, but she represents the SPI brand and makes sure that everyone who comes to the brand gets the handshake they're looking for.

I like my audience to know that I'm listening to them. For instance, I still accept comments on my blog, and try to reply to each one.[3] Although it's become more difficult to do so as my audience has grown, it's a great way to show that I'm actually listening to my audience and interested in what they think about what I've written. Even though a small percentage of people actually leave comments, responding to each person who leaves a comment can make them feel special, like they matter and they weren't wasting their time by stopping by and sharing their thoughts. Plus, even though only a few people may be commenting on a post, many others are seeing these comments, and if my response to another community member is there for everyone to see, that's a positive outcome for the brand as a whole.

However you decide to engage with your audience—I know, for instance, that a lot of blog owners don't accept comments on their posts, which is totally fine and their prerogative—I only ask that you make sure people always know there's another person on the other side of those interactions. Don't leave them out in the cold, no matter what.

When you're small and just starting out, you can use the size of your audience and the simplicity of your business to your advantage. On *SPI Podcast* episode 337, I talked about the advantages of being small, one of which is that you can better connect with your audience. When there are fewer people following you, it's easier to talk to each of them one-on-one. So take the time to reply and reach out individually to everyone who emails or messages you, whether privately or publicly. But you should also take the initial handshake a step further. Keep track of everyone who gets in touch, and follow up with them later. To them, it'll come out of the blue and be completely unexpected, and it'll leave a great impression. They'll think, "Wow, this person hardly even knows me, but they're thinking about me. They took the time to reach back out!" Humans want

---

[3] Read more about my thoughts on blog comments at https://www.smartpassiveincome.com/blog-comments/

to give back to those who give to them, and in many cases, what people want to receive is just a little bit of attention. Give people that extra unexpected attention, and you're going to receive a lot of it back.

I've used this strategy really successfully in my own business. In the early days, when a person commented on my blog, I'd reply to the comment, then I'd go to their website, read their latest article, and comment on the article. Then, I'd send them an email thanking them for the comment and complimenting them on their article, pointing out something specific I enjoyed about it. Although I can't get to every blog comment the same way today, I still use a version of this strategy: often, when a person thanks me for something on social media, I'll send them a direct message via video, thanking them for following my blog or listening to my podcast.

Trust me: people will be bowled over by gestures like this, so give it a shot.

And if you're big, guess what? You can take advantage of the fact that you have systems and resources in place to respond to people and keep track of your interactions so you can follow up with people later. Be the different brand that cares about people, even if they aren't customers yet, and you'll find that you're going to stand out among the crowd like no other.

In later chapters, we'll explore ways to spark the inner superfan in everyone in your audience simply by following up. But for now, know that you'll be on the right track just by meeting every handshake from a new person in your audience with a smile.

EXERCISE

In this exercise, you're going to get better at shaking every hand that comes your way!

STEP 1

Audit your communication channels to find messages you haven't responded to. These could be emails that slipped into your spam folder, blog comments you failed to notice, or Facebook messages you just forgot to answer!

STEP 2

Come up with a system to make sure no more handshakes go unmet and no more messages slip through the cracks. Maybe this means setting aside time on your calendar each week—as little as fifteen minutes—to check all of your inboxes and social media accounts. Or, if the problem requires more time and attention to address, perhaps it's time to hire someone who can help you stay on top of things.

LET'S GO DEEPER

This is an easy way to make a great impression, but sometimes we forget to make it happen. In chapter 5 of your *Superfans* Bonus Companion Course you can discover a few extra things to help make it easier to build a handshake habit that fits into your schedule! Get access at **yoursuperfans.com/course**.

If you want to create an army of superfans, you need to start at the beginning, and that means building paths for casual audience members to become active participants in your brand—subscribers, followers, and regular listeners, viewers, and readers. Thankfully there are many ways you can do that, from learning their language and putting it to use, to creating small, quick wins, sharing who you are, taking people on a journey into the future, and tapping into the simple power of the follow-up.

And trust me—although these strategies represent just the first step to creating superfans, it's so exciting when you see people take that leap from casual visitors to active members of your audience! Each time someone takes that step up, it brings a little more positive energy to your brand and community. Follow the strategies in this first part of the book, and you'll soon be building an audience that's excited to keep hearing from you, one filled with fans who will soon be ready to take the next step: becoming engaged members of your audience who are more closely connected to you and others in the community.

Ready to learn more? Turn the page to part 2, where you'll discover how to start turning this newly active audience into an engaged community.

ACTIVE AUDIENCE TO CONNECTED COMMUNITY

W e're moving on up! In the second part of the book, we'll cover the next climb we need to help the people in our audience take, to move them from an active audience to a connected community.

At the active audience level, people know who you are and have chosen to follow you in some way. That could include joining your email list, following you on social media, subscribing to your podcast, or simply bookmarking your website and checking for updates. When you come out with a new piece of content, or even a new product, each member of your active audience decides whether or not that thing is useful for them or not. They may pass or they may choose to engage with you, but either way, they're still making a choice—an active choice! There's less introduction needed at this phase, since they already know who you are, but there's still work required to get this segment of your audience to take action.

Within the connected community, though, is where voluntary engagement happens. First, there's a connection with you, the owner or creator. Beyond that, and where the magic happens, is the communication and connection between members of the community. The group starts to form its own identity, and members can more easily relate to one another. Within the community, introductions never need to be made from scratch. Simply by being a part of the community, people have an automatic connection point they can use to interact in thoughtful, useful, and memorable ways.

In this part, we'll be covering eight strategies to help you convert your active audience into a highly connected community. We're not quite yet at superfan status yet, but we're on our way, because even at the connected level you're going to see more sharing, more support, and more customers. As you navigate the strategies in this second stage of superfan building, there's a key principle that ties everything together, one that will help you take those active fans to the next level as members of an engaged community:

People want to feel like they belong.

Back in high school, I had the honor of being one of the shortest kids in my entire grade. Just to give you some perspective, I didn't pass 5 feet tall (about 1.5 meters) until senior year. I played the trumpet in the marching band, not just because it was a cool instrument, but because most of the other instruments I wanted to play were, well, almost as big as I was.

As the shortest kid, I did get picked on a little, mostly verbal abuse here and there. It didn't feel good, but thankfully my friends were always there to back me up. I was fortunate to surround myself with friends who stood up for me. Unfortunately, their favorite sport was basketball.

After school, the guys and I would hang out before band practice and shoot hoops on the playground. And every time, it was always the same. I was last to be picked, I never got passed the ball, and therefore I never got a chance to shoot. I was on the court, but I wasn't really playing. It was never that much fun for me.

One year, some of the guys decided to participate in a three-on-three tournament at San Diego State University and invited the rest of us to come watch. When they asked if I wanted going to join them, I said no. They asked why, and here's what I said:

"You guys let me play, but I never even get to touch the ball. I don't have fun playing basketball, so why would I want to go and watch?"

When it comes to building community, make sure you're just not inviting people onto the basketball court, but that you're also passing them the ball from time to time. I tell you, if I'd been passed the ball every once in a while, if I'd had the opportunity to shoot the ball from time to time, I would have gladly joined the fellas and watched the tournament. I wouldn't have expected to play (for obvious reasons), but I would have done what I could to help the team win. I'd have made sure the water bottles were full all the time, I'd have handed out towels during timeouts and halftime, and I would have screamed as loudly as I could in support of them.

But nope. I didn't feel like it.

This part of the book is all about how to build community by making people feel like they belong and getting them engaged. They follow you and know you exist, but now you need to invite them onto the court with you. Pass them the ball every once in a while, and give them a chance to score.

- ▶ **CHAPTER 6: LET THEM TAKE A SHOT**
- ▶ **CHAPTER 7: LET THEM DECIDE**
- ▶ **CHAPTER 8: CREATE A CHALLENGE**
- ▶ **CHAPTER 9: OPEN THE FACTORY DOORS**
- ▶ **CHAPTER 10: STAGE A GIG**
- ▶ **CHAPTER 11: GIVE THEM A NAME**
- ▶ **CHAPTER 12: BRING THEM TOGETHER**
- ▶ **CHAPTER 13: MAKE THEM SHINE**

It's time to create a team worth rooting for, so let's get right into it . . .

LET THEM TAKE A SHOT

S teve Spangler is a scientist and an entertainer. In other words, he's *awesome*, and my favorite kind of person. I first saw him on the *Ellen Degeneres Show*, performing some amazing experiments for her audience. My favorite was one where he shot clouds of ring-shaped smoke out of a large plastic trash can. You may also know him as the originator of the Mentos and Diet Coke video trend. (Look it up!)

One day, to my surprise, I heard Steve being interviewed on one of my favorite podcasts, *The Social Media Marketing Podcast*, hosted by my good friend Michael Stelzner. I thought to myself, "What's Steve doing on Mike's social media podcast?"

Little did I know, this would be a game-changing interview for my business.

Steve told the story about how he started his YouTube channel, *Sick Science*, in 2007. Before then, he'd been posting YouTube videos with cool science experiments that got lots of views but little in the way of engagement. In the podcast interview, he describes just how sad the engagement was on his videos at the beginning:

> "The . . . videos that we had already had up on YouTube
> prior to Sick Science averaged probably between six and

> ten comments, and many of those were 'First!' or 'Cool science!' or just some sort of horrible comment, right?"

His audience engagement was meager and low quality. Even with a sizable group of subscribers who watched all his videos, they weren't giving him much in terms of action beyond what they came there for.

So Steve and his team made a small tweak that made a massive difference when it came to engagement on the videos: Instead of revealing how the science worked, they added a question to the end of the video description that invited people to explain how they thought the experiment worked. Here's how Steve describes this shift:

> "The question at the end is what made the huge change for YouTube, and that is: 'In the comments below, tell us how you think this works.' Ba-dum! That's it."

Can you guess what happened next? Engagement went through the roof! Simply by asking for the answer—the science behind the experiments he was showing—he gave more power to his audience to step up and participate. He let them shoot their shot, and boy did they shoot.

> "As soon as we put up Sick Science, I believe that first video that we put up had 850 comments. And 850 engaging comments, where people . . . were saying, 'The reason the egg went in the bottle was because of this,' and they would lay out how that works."

The strategy worked like gangbusters. Tons of people began to comment on each new video with their best version of the right answer. They instigated friendly debates within the comments section. Some comments would get a bunch of likes and climb to the top. At times, it turned into an all-out war of hypotheses.

All this engagement was a game-changer for Steve and *Sick Science*. Here's Steve again on what it did for him and his channel:

> "And it was truly that level of engagement, not the number of hits, that got YouTube's attention that

> ultimately led to the offer we were given to be one of
> the 100 funded channels."

Steve is referring to the title YouTube bestowed on him as one of their "100 Original Content Providers"—a pretty amazing honor, and one Steve attributes directly to his "let them shoot their shot" engagement strategy.

Big crowds draw people in. When you see a large crowd of people hovering around something, your natural instinct is to find out what's grabbing their attention. And you can use this instinct to engage your audience, create a crowd, and get people to look your way and join in. People will come back to continue conversations they've started with each other. Once they're in, they're in, and they're going to want to keep those conversations going (especially if they're getting notifications every time someone replies to a thread). And with social media platforms rewarding engagement, you're going to see more people discovering your content and interacting with it as a result.

The crux of this strategy is to ask your audience for an answer—even if you already know it yourself. Now, you might be worried that by asking for an answer it may seem like you don't know the answer yourself. That's not true. You're simply allowing your audience to talk amongst each other, which you may find to be valuable, not just for the reasons above, but because—guess what—your audience likely knows a thing or two! You and the rest of the community can learn from each other and have healthy debates about things. Your role is to foster a safe environment for this to happen, one that would be hard for people to find elsewhere. This will help people feel like they're a part of something they can relate to, not just because you're there creating the environment to allow this to happen, but because people are now able to find people who are just as passionate about the topic as they are (or more!).

Just for fun, ask your audience on social media (it doesn't matter what your target audience is) this question:

Which one is healthier: kale, or spinach?

If you wanted to grab a little bit more attention, attach an animated gif along with it. You're going to see people scramble to give you their best answer, many of them so scientific that you'll know they spent a half-hour researching on Wikipedia. Some people, however, will give you only one-word answers, and that's okay too, because they'll still feel like they have a voice, and that's really important to belonging. You're giving them a reason to use that voice.

These conversations always work best if you choose a topic that's related to your audience, but it doesn't need to be that way. Here's an example of one of my most engaged posts on Instagram in terms of number of comments and likes in the shortest time period:

Or another example I love, the Instagram account for the TV show *The Walking Dead* asking a "What would you do?" question to engage their audience:

This strategy is beautiful because it's about letting people in and allowing them to tell part of the brand's story. It's like inviting your entire audience into your "writers' room," where they can share their opinions on where the story should go—and connect with each other in that process of storytelling. It also works really well when you ask people to answer a question that doesn't have an obvious, "correct" answer. When *The Walking Dead*'s Instagram team asks the show's fans to decide how the show's story arc should go, they're not looking for a right answer—by making the question intentionally ambiguous, with no clear answer, they're going to spark people to engage and stand up for why they think one outcome is better than the other.

The next strategy takes the Let Them Take a Shot method a step further, by allowing your fans to play a more active role in your brand and actually help influence your next steps. That's right—it's time to let them decide.

EXERCISE

See what it's like to give your audience a chance to take a shot.

STEP 1

On your favorite social media account, ask a question that you already know the answer to. It can be related to your business, but it doesn't have to be. If you can support the choice with an image or video, even better.

STEP 2

Don't take it too seriously. Experiment, have fun, and see what works best for your audience.

LET'S GO DEEPER

For more inspiration and examples to help fuel your audience participation, check out chapter 6 of your *Superfans* Bonus Companion Course at **yoursuperfans.com/course**.

CHAPTER 07

LET THEM DECIDE

C *uusoo* is a Japanese word that means *fantasy* or *imagination*. It's also the inspiration behind CUUSOO SYSTEM, a Japanese company that was formed in 1997 as a platform for crowdfunding new products and connecting product creators with manufacturers. In 2008, CUUSOO SYSTEM formed a partnership with LEGO to create LEGO CUUSOO, a dream for anyone who has ever played with LEGO before.

Imagine this: designing and building your own unique LEGO structure—anything your imagination can come up with—and then having LEGO actually manufacture your design as an official LEGO product and selling it in stores. They'll even give you 1 percent of the royalties from sales. This is what LEGO CUUSOO, now known as LEGO IDEAS, does. It's an entire platform built to allow LEGO creators to help shape the product line and get their creations made. The process is pretty straightforward: If a design gets at least ten thousand votes from LEGO's online community, it becomes eligible to potentially be manufactured as a real LEGO product. How amazing is that?!

Several products created by regular people—non-employees—have been manufactured and sold by LEGO, from a Minecraft set in 2012 to a set highlighting the Women of NASA in 2017, and my all-time favorite, from 2013, the DeLorean from *Back to the Future*. Although this was not my design (and I wish it had been), it still makes me appreciate LEGO even more knowing it was something a fellow fan like me created. Just the fact that LEGO is listening is huge for community growth, because instead of a one-sided conversation, it's something anyone can participate in.

The former CEO of LEGO, Jørgen Vig Knudstorp, was quoted in a 2009 *Harvard Business Review* article sharing the wonders of allowing the brand's community of fans to contribute to product design: "While we have 120 staff designers, we potentially have probably 120,000 volunteer designers we can access outside the company to help us invent."[4] LEGO understands that not all of the best ideas come internally, and that by calling on their customers, their fans, it can create things its audience already wants. Like many great brands, LEGO encourages interaction and wants its audience to suggest product ideas.

This process is known as co-creation, and it's a brilliant way to further activate your audience and turn them into a connected community. Many other companies, from Unilever to DeWalt to DHL and General Mills have seen the benefit of turning to their customers for insights into building effective products and services. And when you ask your fans for advice, then follow through on that advice, they're going to see that and appreciate it.

Speaking of LEGO, the company's ranks of superfans have been instrumental in its success—especially because not too long ago, it was massively in debt (to the tune of $800 million in 2003) and on the brink of bankruptcy. With a shift to focusing on what its fans really want, LEGO has since rebounded and as of 2018 was the largest toy company in the world with a valuation of $7.6 billion, higher than massive brands like Mattel or Hasbro![5]

But what if you're not a giant company with the resources to create a crowdsourced platform like LEGO IDEAS? How can you get your

---

[4] Andrew O'Connell, "Lego CEO Jørgen Vig Knudstorp on leading through survival and growth," *Harvard Business Review*, (Jan 2009), https://hbr.org/2009/01/lego-ceo-jorgen-vig-knudstorp-on-leading-through-survival-and-growth.

[5] Lucy Handley, "How marketing built Lego into the world's favorite toy brand," *CNBC*, (Apr 27, 2018), https://www.cnbc.com/2018/04/27/lego-marketing-strategy-made-it-world-favorite-toy-brand.html.

audience to level up and feel like they're a part of something? How can you engage with that audience to co-create the products and solutions they crave?

It's not as hard as you might think, and you already have access to the tools to make it happen.

Amy Porterfield is one of the smartest people I know. A successful entrepreneur and an amazing friend, I've been inspired by her for years. Her branding is flawless, her podcast is top-notch, and her audience of raving fans will follow her to the moon, which is exactly why when I saw the Facebook post she published on June 20, 2013, I was a little surprised:

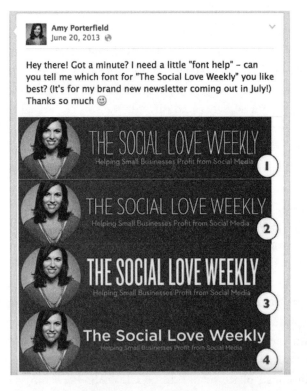

A little "font help"? Amy has people who do this kind of work for her, so why is she asking her audience for "font help"? Because, like I said, she's one of the smartest people I know.

Involving her audience in this decision *isn't* about the final outcome. The decision on which email header to use isn't going to change any lives or affect her business in a meaningful way. Instead, it's about participation and communication. The word *communication*, in fact, derives from the Latin word *communis*, which means *common*, or *sharing*. Similarly, the word *community* means *same*. Without communication, there is no community.

Going back to Amy's example, how did this perform? It was one of her most engaging posts in months. People love to vote, participate, and get involved, and after seeing her example, I immediately created something similar and posted it on my Facebook Page. It was a side-by-side of two logos for a new design for a niche site I had built in the security guard training industry.

Same results! It was the most engaged post I'd ever had. It amassed over one thousand comments, while my second most commented post had fewer than three hundred. As a side benefit to this type of strategy, you can expect Facebook and other social media platforms to reward you for higher engagement in your posts, which is exactly what they want. Oh, and of course, you can also gauge the answers to see which one people actually do like better. Sometimes it's split, and other times there's a clear winner.

I used this strategy again in 2016 when working on my book *Will It Fly? How to Test Your Next Business Idea Before You Waste Your Time and*

Money. I shared various designs of the book cover with my audience to see which one people liked best, and again, it became the most engaged post of the year.

Letting your audience help influence your business isn't something new, but it's something everyone can easily do. Have a YouTube channel? Ask your viewers what your next videos should be about, just like *Epic Rap Battles of History*. This YouTube show, which features actors portraying two famous people having a rap battle together, shows screenshots from commenters who have helped to influence each new video they create. At the end of each video, they ask, "Who's next? You decide."

Writing a book? I'm not the only one who has thought to bring their audience along for the ride. Andy Weir involved his small audience on his blog by publicly writing, chapter by chapter, a story about a man stuck on Mars. The story began to get noticed, and his audience began to give feedback and suggestions about the content in his story. Eventually this series of blog posts turned into a bestselling book, *The Martian*, which later became a film starring Matt Damon.

Own a candy company? Have your consumers help select the next big flavor and vote, just like Mars did in 1995 when it replaced the tan-colored M&M's after people voted by calling 1-800-FUN-COLOR.

Make things people can use or wear? Have your audience tell you what to make. Betabrand is a clothing manufacturer that, like LEGO, takes letting them decide to another level. First, the company allows designers to submit proposals for new products publicly. If a proposal is accepted, audience members vote on it. If it gets the thumbs up, the garment becomes available for pre-order. If it receives enough pre-orders, it goes into production! And here's the amazing part: The designer receives 10 percent of all sales in the first year. Most of Betabrand's clothing is designed to solve a particular problem, especially for travel (such as with hidden passport pockets or being reversible to allow for multiple looks from a single garment), and crowdsourcing the design of many of those products is a great way Betabrand ensures that those products meet their customers' needs.

Whatever your focus, crowdsourcing can work for you. I've used this strategy successfully in other ways in my own business. I've asked my Twitter fans who to interview on my podcast. And I've asked students in the beta testing group for each new course for feedback on what's missing or could be improved, then putting that feedback right back into the course. Here's the great part: in all of these examples, I'm not just asking my audience questions I already know the answer to. I'm gaining real knowledge and insight in the process, learning what people want from me and my brand.

So how can you get your audience involved? You don't need to make them the CEO of your company or let them dictate every single decision. As you can see, giving your audience a chance to speak up on even small decisions can get them excited to be involved and engaged.

Fans love it when you give them a chance to be a part of the decision-making process—it makes them feel like part of the brand, part of a family, which ultimately leads to feeling more connected to you and the community that you're fostering. Our next strategy is about creating a space in your brand community where people feel challenged and excited to make positive changes in their own lives, and excited to share that progress with the rest of the community.

EXERCISE

Give your audience a chance to vote or make a decision in your business.

STEP 1

The choice you offer doesn't have to be what the next product will be (although in the end all of your products should be a result of what best serves your audience), but a simple "this or that" question can be one that would allow your audience to feel like a part of the process.

STEP 2

If you can, support it with a "this or that" image, showing one versus another, and make it easy for people to vote and leave their opinion. (Hint: polls on Instagram stories is a great way to do this!)

STEP 3

Remember that you'll make the ultimate decision, of course, but it's a fun way to get your audience involved.

BONUS TIP

This is a great strategy for when you feel stuck making a decision, or anything that you and your team would have an internal brainstorm session about.

CREATE A CHALLENGE

You may remember this next strategy from part 1, when I talked about how I help people achieve a small, quick win through my "100 Email Challenge." Challenges, when done effectively, are so powerful that they're well worth bringing back into the conversation when you're trying to turn your active audience into a connected community.

Jadah Sellner and Jen Hansard are the founders of Simple Green Smoothies, a truly exciting online business that's transforming the health of its community. In 2008, Jadah and Jen were both stay-at-home moms with a dream of going into business together. After discovering the awesome power of green smoothies to transform personal health, Jadah and Jen decided to write an ebook to share their knowledge, and Simple Green Smoothies was born.

Four hundred thousand Instagram followers, two best-selling cookbooks, and a top-rated recipe app later, Simple Green Smoothies engages a massive community of passionate fans. And the biggest way they drive that engagement is through their free 30-day green smoothie challenges.

In these challenges, subscribers receive a weekly email with five smoothie recipes and a shopping list for the week. These challenges are a way to invite casual fans to become subscribers. But they're also a way to rapidly turn those subscribers into engaged members of the community. As new subscribers shop for their green smoothies and acclimate to what, for many of them, is a radical new way of eating, Jadah and Jen's team provides real-time motivation and facilitates connection with other challenge members who may be having a similar experience. Here's how Jadah describes it to me on *SPI Podcast* episode 205:

> "For thirty days, we are actually in this with you. Our community happiness specialist, Jen, and I, we're responding to all of the comments. We are engaging with our community; we are cheering them on and we are like all hands on deck, like every email, every comment that is posted on Facebook and Instagram, we are answering their questions or we're in it for this set time. It is committing to, 'Here is the start day and here is the end day, and we are in this together.'"

In fact, Jen and Jadah made a conscious decision to emphasize the community-building aspects of their challenges over the opportunity to make more money from them. They fully realize the income potential they're giving up on by maintaining the hands-on support and community aspect of their challenges. As Jadah says, "We have definitely thought about like, 'Oh, we should package this and sell it and just have it going all the time, but kind of the secret magic to our challenge is that the community engagement that it's live and it's in real time."

In your business and your brand, you'll be faced with moments where you can choose to make things more automated, or more human. There's often not a "right" or "wrong" choice in these situations, but if you're trying to build an engaged community of people on their way to becoming superfans, then erring on the side of human will take you a long way. In Jadah and Jen's challenges, the brand and audience are, as Jadah puts it, "in it together as a community":

> "You can't automate connection and outsource authenticity, and not to say that you can't transform someone's life through automating things, but I think

> there's something special when you are in it in real time. We're sending those emails. We can automate schedules when the email will go out each week, but we're just in it together as a community from the start date to the end date, and that's how we are able to fully show up with them in that time."

The thirty-day green smoothie challenges provide participants with a community to latch onto, along with motivation and accountability to achieve their goal of changing their relationship to food by simply having a daily smoothie for a month.

But that's not the only thing that makes these challenges work for the Simple Green Smoothies community. Jadah and Jen also do one more crucial thing that helps make their challenges even more successful at motivating people to participate and engage: They run the challenge just four times a year, which creates excitement and a sense of scarcity. People can't access the challenge whenever they like, which makes it special—but they also know when it'll come back around, which means they can anticipate and plan for it.

Fun fact: the first draft of this book was written as part of one of the most popular and successful challenges out there, one you may have heard of: the National Novel Writing Month (NaNoWriMo) challenge! Every November, this nonprofit organization challenges writers around the world to take one month to write the first draft of their novel—at least fifty thousand words. But NaNoWriMo doesn't just let these writers loose into the wild to come up with a novel all by themselves. The organization maintains a forum on its website where writers can go to get support and inspiration as they're slogging through their draft. The brand also has a presence on practically all the social media platforms—Facebook, Twitter, Tumblr, YouTube, Instagram, and Pinterest—where authors also congregate and interact.

And those authors definitely take advantage of this community support—in fact, as I was writing this chapter in March 2019, I visited the NaNoWriMo forums, where a little label near the bottom of the page told me there were currently "114,466 users online." That's right: more than one hundred thousand people were engaged in the forums for a November novel writing challenge, almost as far away from November as you can get.

Although I didn't engage with the NaNoWriMo community on the organization's forums or social media channels while I was writing, I did share my progress with my audience through a daily word count tracker in an Excel sheet. It was an awesome way to connect my community to my personal writing process, and tons of people cheered me on and helped hold me accountable for getting my draft done.

NaNoWriMo is also just an awesome organization that I'm happy to support, especially because they run several programs to support writing in local communities, including the Young Writers Program, which promotes writing in K-12 classrooms, a "virtual writing retreat" called Camp NaNoWriMo, and the Come Write In program, which provides free resources to libraries, community centers, and bookstores to build local "writing havens." And they're able to support these causes because of the community of storytelling superfans they've built, a community that exists because NaNoWriMo has mastered the art of tapping into two really powerful human impulses: the need to write and tell our stories, and the desire to meet a challenge with everything we've got.

Finally, a fun example that shows challenges don't need to be elaborate to be effective. The car company MINI has their own long-running challenge, and it's based around a simple hashtag: #FitsInMyMINI. Every month, the brand challenges owners of its famously small but fun cars to see what they can fit inside, then take a picture and share it on social media. The winning selection each month gets posted on MINI's Instagram account. The prize for winning the challenge—recognition on social media—is simple but powerful at spurring people to engage with the brand.

When you create a space for someone to succeed in a supportive community of others trying to do the same, you're giving them a great way to reach their goals and become a tight-knit member of the clan. The next strategy is based on the magic of opening the factory doors—taking people behind the scenes and tapping into the shared human fascination for how things work.

EXERCISE

Come up with a challenge for your audience. It doesn't have to be complicated, and it doesn't have to be huge. It should be achievable but—yes—a little challenging.

STEP 1

Brainstorm your challenge. Here are some questions to help get you thinking:

- What are activities related to your brand that will bring people together?
- How long should the challenge be? (My 100 Email Challenge is just three days. Some challenges can be less than an hour.)
- When will you host the challenge, and how frequently? Is it a one-time thing, or ongoing?

STEP 2

Decide how you'll deliver the challenge. Will it be through daily emails? Videos hosted on your website? Or instructions delivered in a series of daily messages or livestreams on social media?

STEP 3

Decide how you'll facilitate community engagement. You'll need a place for people to discuss the challenge and provide support and inspiration, such as a Facebook group, or a hashtag for Instagram and Twitter.

STEP 4

Announce and host your challenge!

LET'S GO DEEPER

Running challenges can be difficult, but they can make a world of difference if executed well. Be sure to check out the extra resources to help you structure your first challenge in chapter 8 of your *Superfans* Bonus Companion Course at **yoursuperfans.com/course**.

OPEN THE FACTORY DOORS

H umans have always had a fascination for how things work. Curiosity has been a constant part of who we are, so when given the opportunity, we gravitate toward knowing something rather than not. On each episode of the television show *How It's Made*, the hosts take you inside a factory to literally show you how different things are made! The first episode came out in February 2001, and thirty-one seasons and more than four hundred episodes later, the show is still going strong.

During the American industrial revolution in the eighteenth century, factories started to spring up as production processes shifted from handmade to machine made. In 1790, the first factory was built in America, a cotton-spinning mill in Pawtucket, Rhode Island. Over the next several decades, thousands more would pop up across the country. Back then, factories tended to be very secretive about their processes. Doors were largely closed except to factory workers and investors involved in the business.

But in the late 1890s, something funny happened. As more and more products were being mass-produced in a mechanized way—things like cars, appliances, even food—people started to become fascinated by how those things were made. They wanted to be closer to the action.

Those factory-held secrets started to find an audience as factory owners, recognizing the appeal, began opening their doors to public tours. No longer was everything happening behind the scenes; now people, especially families, could spend their leisure time visiting factories and stepping into the wonderful world of how the things they used and enjoyed in their daily lives were made.

Today, factory tours happen every day, all over the world, across all business types. You can walk through the Hershey's factory in Hershey, Pennsylvania, to see exactly how the company's famous Kisses come off the line (seventy million a day across the company's two factories!), walk amongst giant brew kettles at your favorite brewery or distillery, or even take a backlot bus tour through some of Hollywood's iconic sets and soundstages (including, yes, *Back to the Future*).

Why is the factory tour—whether it happens in real life or on a TV show like *How It's Made*—such a draw? It provides four things people want to see and experience, factors that can help turn active audience members into engaged fans of your connected community.

1. It Helps Your Audience Appreciate the Quality and Care Behind the Product

When you see how things are made, you feel great about the brand and its effort to make sure things are up to standard. The families that lined up to visit factories in the early twentieth century weren't necessarily doing so to oversee the quality of the products being made, but when they saw the care and precision put into the creation of each product, it left a lasting impression.

When Apple came out with the unibody version of its MacBook Pro laptop computer in 2008—a unique design that used a single piece of aluminum to create the computer's casing—it also took its fans behind the scenes of the creation of this impressive engineering feat. Rather than just describing the process in a blog post, Apple released a video describing the philosophy and process behind the unibody MacBook Pro's design, featuring interviews with Jony Ive, Apple's famous design head, and Dan Riccio, the company's VP of product design, as well as footage of the unibody being precision-crafted from a huge aluminum block in one of Apple's factories. The video really drove home the care and ingenuity Apple put into creating this product.

When you open your factory doors, your fans will appreciate the love and care you put into the things you create for them.

2. It Makes Your Audience Feel Unique and Special

One weekend in college, I took a tour of the Scharffen Berger Chocolate Factory, which was close to the UC Berkeley campus. I hadn't even heard of Scharffen Berger before that weekend, but after seeing their chocolate-making process, getting a little morsel of chocolate education, and meeting the friendly staff, I had an experience I'll remember for life. Now, whenever I see a wall of chocolate bars for sale at the store, I zero in on Scharffen Berger, remember my tour, and pick up a bar.

Building a tribe of superfans is about creating special moments and experiences. Not everyone is going to get to take a factory tour or see what goes on behind the scenes, and that's what makes these moments even more special for people who do get to experience them. By gaining some inside knowledge and seeing things other people don't, people begin to feel closer to the brand. They start to inch away from the crowd of "normal" people who don't know or care as much about your brand, and to connect with other people who "get it" when it comes to the brand.

When you open your factory doors, your fans will feel like they've been given something not everyone has access to.

3. It Connects Your Audience with the People Behind the Brand

People *buy* solutions, but they *connect* with other people. Opening up your factory doors and connecting your audience to the people behind the product is a crucial way to build superfans. In the Break the Ice strategy from part 1, we talked about why you should share a little bit about yourself to create a personal connection with your audience, but this is more than that. It's about sharing the other people who normally don't get seen—the people, literally, behind the scenes.

For some businesses, it may be featuring the people who are literally on the factory floor. Diana Hunter, for example, was the beloved "Honey Bunches of Oats" lady who had been working at the Post cereal brand for forty years. In 2015, she started appearing in television commercials filmed on the factory floor in Battle Creek, Michigan, where she worked. She had a charm that people fell in love with, and it made people feel closer to the brand—so much so that when she retired, it was a big news story.

E! News ✓
@enews

The best of the bunch has moved on—The Honey Bunches of Oats lady retired after more than 40 years. eonli.ne/2gS2crW

♡ 18.6K 9:02 PM - Sep 9, 2017

♡ 5,851 people are talking about this   >

Then there are people like Coyote Peterson, a YouTuber with over twelve million subscribers on his channel, *Brave Wilderness*, who is known for his educational and sometimes shocking wildlife videos. His "insect bite" videos are his most popular, where he demonstrates on his own body just how painful these bites can be. It's not just shock and awe, though. He does a great job educating his viewers, mainly young children, about the respect we need to give these animals and the dangers they present.

Coyote is definitely the main character in his videos, but fans have also grown to love his cameramen, Mario and Mark, who get out from behind the lens from time to time and appear on the show. I took my kids to see Coyote Peterson live when he was on tour in San Diego, and when Coyote and his crew came on stage, my son exclaimed, "Mark and Mario are here too!"

It's always great to know the people behind the things we love, whether they're products, shows, or stories. Remember, people connect with people.

When you open your factory doors, your fans will cherish the opportunity to see and connect with the people behind the brand.

4. It Gives Your Audience Something to Share

I remember watching Pixar's *Toy Story* in 1995 and loving it. Then in 2000, the DVD came out so I could watch it at home, and I bought it immediately. Although it was great to relive the movie and the characters that I and millions of others had fallen in love with, it was the bonus section of the DVD that became my new favorite thing. It included the following options:

The Making of Toy Story took me into Pixar's amazing quest to create the first ever completely computer-animated full feature film. It was a roller coaster of a timeline that involved the success of *Tin Toy (1988)*, an award-winning animated short that experimented with the technology, Steve Jobs buying Pixar, Disney coming on board to support the film only to later almost pull the plug because they were unhappy with the story development, to Tom Hanks, Tim Allen, and the other memorable voices of the movie. It was the most amazing thing I had ever seen.

I won't go into detail about the background of *Toy Story*,[6] but I'll tell you what I did as soon as I learned all of these amazing facts about the movie: I shared them with everyone I knew.

When you know something other people don't, unless you're sworn to secrecy, you tell others. It's why gossip is so popular, why people who aren't from California who visit their friends always hear about In-N-Out Burger's secret menu, and why when you know a bunch of random facts about a company or movie you love, a lot of your conversations with your friends and followers tend to start with, "Did you know that … "

When you open your factory doors, your fans will want to share the things they learn about you with others.

In October 2008, after launching an ebook study guide for architects studying for the LEED exam, I created *The Smart Passive Income Blog*, a new website to keep track of my progress as I began to build my business and figure things out. It became a platform for me to share everything I was learning along the way, including all of my wins, and all of my failures, too.

In November 2008, I decided to try something I was inspired to do by a blog in the personal finance space, MyMoneyBlog.com. The author of this blog would openly share his portfolio breakdown and investment results over time. It was incredibly helpful to see, and also super inspiring to me as someone who was saving for the future. As a new business owner, I thought it would be helpful to my audience to share how much income I was generating, so I published my very first income report on my blog.

The report included information about what I had recently been doing in my business, from joining an online course, to launching my new ebook. The most popular part of the post, however, was the income breakdown itself:

---

[6] If you want to learn more, I recommend reading Ed Catmull's book *Creativity, Inc.*

Income Breakdown

		DIFFERENCE FROM LAST MONTH	
GROSS INCOME	$7,906.55	$7,906.55	0%
NICHE SITES	$7,906.55	$0.00	
Green Exam Academy eBook Sales	$7,126.91	$0.00	%
Green Exam Academy Google Adsense	$596.31	$0.00	%
Green Exam Academy Private Advertising	$183.33	$0.00	%

This wasn't the first time someone in the internet marketing space had shared their numbers, but for the small group of people who were visiting my blog, it was eye-opening. Suddenly, they started commenting and sharing the report with their followers and friends. I began to notice the traffic on my website starting to climb, too. Then, in December, when I published November's report, which showed a 23 percent gross jump in online income, more and more people started to come on board. By opening the factory doors, I had created an opportunity for my active audience, the people who were already reading the reports but not yet sharing them, to become much more connected and engaged.

For nearly ten years, I published income reports on my blog each month, often with an annual report to go along with them. Those articles have become my most visited blog posts ever, and in 2012 I was recognized by *Forbes* in an article titled "10 Leaders Who Aren't Afraid to Be Transparent," alongside other entrepreneurs such as Tony Hsieh of Zappos, Jason Fried of 37signals, and other amazing business leaders.

I say this not to show off, but to show you what can happen when you're transparent and share a bit about what happens behind the scenes. You don't need to tell people how much money you make if you don't want to, but sharing your progress and your journey along the way can go a long way in building an amazing tribe of loyal fans that gets access to special insights about you and your business.

In fact, it can be as simple as giving people a glimpse of where you work. Something I've done on a couple occasions is a video tour of the places I work. In 2015, I shared a video of my home office workspace. Then in 2017, I posted another video tour of the studio where I used to record all my live video. Each time I got tons of great comments from people who called out various aspects of the tour they appreciated and even shared details of their own workspaces.

Sharing more of who you are and what you do with your customers and soon-to-be customers can go a long way in making your audience more engaged! As a brand, as a creator, as a company, you need to harness the human love for seeing how things are made, because by doing so, you'll build a stronger brand and a more connected community. Take your active audience behind the scenes to give them a glimpse of how your brand works and foster their love for connecting with you and others in the community.

From here, we take to the stage! It's time to put on your first gig, and start engaging your active audience through the magic of a live event, one that brings people together in a unique atmosphere of excitement and connection.

EXERCISE

Share something related to your business that you've never shared with your audience before.

STEP 1

Share something behind the curtain or behind the scenes that will be super interesting for people to know about how you and your team do what you do!

STEP 2

Experiment and have fun seeing the results of trying something new.

BONUS TIP

If possible, try to open your doors related to something trackable each month! This will keep your audience hooked and excited to see how things progress over time. For me, this was my income reports, but you don't have to share income for it to be interesting. Perhaps it's miles ran, or carbon emissions avoided, or how much debt paid off. These types of numbers, especially when related to your business, are inspiring and definitely make people feel special for knowing insider info!

STAGE A GIG

On August 8, 1998, during a warm summer night at the Universal Amphitheater in Los Angeles, California, April attended her first Backstreet Boys concert with her best friend. April's brother had gifted her two tickets for her birthday, after a year in which her obsession with the group had become abundantly clear.

Every day for months, April and her friend looked forward to the concert with great anticipation. Months ahead of the concert, the two of them talked daily at school about the songs they were hoping to hear, the dances they might see on stage, and even what clothes they were going to wear. As the date got closer, they got more and more hyped up, and their love for the band grew even more. Just the chance to see them live was a dream about to come true.

And of course, the concert was awesome. I know this because April was able to recall that night vividly when we chatted about it a mere twenty years later. She remembered the stage design, the songs, and of course, her boys. But she'd seen them and heard their songs thousands of times before on television and on the radio. Why would the concert have been any different?

For anyone who's ever attended a live concert, you know the answer: It's a whole new level of awesome. The real-life live setting, the crowd there for the exact same reasons you are—it's a feeling you can't capture in any other way.

This is why when you're a brand, whether that means a musician who plays songs or a business that builds products and solutions, creating events like this—what I like to call *gigs*—can be a game-changing strategy for the growth and strength of your community. If you want to take your audience from active to connected, you've got to be willing to gig.

I like the word *gig* because it's a little less intimidating than something like *concert* or *event*. You don't have to spend hundreds of thousands of dollars for set design and A/V in order to pull off the same thing musicians do while on tour. All you need is a time, a location, and enough prep time to let people know you're going to show up, live. A gig!

Gigs can also take many forms. You could host a training workshop at a local coworking space for a small group of people. You could get a booth on the expo floor during a conference in your niche market to show off your product. Or you could speak on stage at an event. And gigs don't have to happen live and in person—they can happen live and online, too.

When I started blogging, one of the first resources I found was Darren Rowse's ProBlogger.net. I read Darren's blog every single day, and as soon as I heard he was going to do a special video live stream with chat, I was quick to register. I marked it on the calendar, and like April's BSB concert, it was something I was totally looking forward to. (April might disagree that my live stream ended up being as exciting as her concert, but I digress.) I planned to stay up really late that night because of the time zone difference between the US and Australia, which is where Darren is from. This was something I didn't want to miss!

When the time finally came, I signed on and was placed in a waiting room with a bunch of other people I'd never met before. There were a few hundred of us, and we were able to have a conversation with each other in the chat room before the event started, which was really cool. Then, all of a sudden, Darren's face appeared on the screen. There he was, streaming from his home in Melbourne!

He shared some updates about his blog, along with a number of helpful tips and strategies, which was great, but what I found to be the most exciting portion of the show was the question-and-answer segment. Sifting through the busy comment stream, Darren found interesting questions, mentioned that person's name, and then shared his thoughts. After trying multiple times to be seen in the comment stream, I was almost about to give up when, all of a sudden, I heard Darren say: "Here's a question from Patrick."

That was me! It was my full name, which I used when signing up for the software, but he read my question in full and proceeded to answer it. As he was answering my question, I was looking right at him, and he was looking directly at me. At least that's how it felt. I know he was just looking into his webcam, but still—I really felt like he was there in the room with me.

From that point on, I developed a serious affinity for Darren and the ProBlogger community. A couple of years later, I got to meet him at a conference, and we've since become great friends. I've even been to Australia to speak on his stage at his ProBlogger events, and to this day I remain a huge fan of him and his work.

Small events can go a long way, especially if you do them regularly. Today, it's easier than ever to pull off something similar to what Darren did. With Facebook Live, YouTube Live, Twitch, Periscope, and other live streaming software, you can bring your community together and strengthen the bonds they have with you and each other. And unlike a live, in-person event, these online events can also be shared with audiences you haven't even tapped into yet.

By the way, these kinds of events are powerful on their own, but there are little things you can do to amplify their effect. As a tip, whenever possible, make sure you do your best to call out people's names. This creates a trigger that makes people feel instantly connected to you. It's just like at a restaurant when your server uses your name (which we'll talk more about in chapter 14)—it's different, and it's special.

Bigger events, although much harder to coordinate, can also do wonders for growing a community. The trouble is there are a lot of moving pieces, from venue space, to audio/visual elements, to ticketing, design work, food and catering, travel and lodging, insurance, etc. It's a lot. But the experience, if those pieces are put together in the right way, can be epic. Chalene Johnson, a fitness trainer and business coach from Southern California you might remember from the "Break the Ice" strategy in part 1, is also a mentor of mine who has put on several incredible live events for her tribe. One of them is called Marketing Impact Academy, and the other is the Smart Success Seminar. I've had the privilege of speaking at both of these events, and every time I've been blown away. The excitement, the energy, the emotion—I've never seen anything like it. You can't get that in an online room; it's the kind of thing that can only happen in person. I've honestly never spoken in front of a more energized crowd, which pumps me up when I'm on stage too, of course!

Chalene's events were so inspiring to me that I decided to use her effort as a model and put on my own live event in San Diego called FlynnCon, which started in 2019. In fact, this very book you're reading right this moment was launched at the very first FlynnCon, something I gave away as a gift for everyone who attended the event![7]

Putting on an event, big or small, can be a little nerve-racking. It's live, so you actually have to interact and be present, and truly care about the experience of the end user. But, don't worry—going live, especially online, is not as scary as you might think—and this is coming from someone who avoided the stage and even online streaming for years because I was so scared. Now, it's something I do regularly. Online, people usually won't expect you to have everything nailed down. In fact, sometimes it's the random occurrences, like kids in the background or random things falling off the wall, that make those streams more special. It's closer to real life, and that's what will make people love you even more.

The last thing, before you execute on this, is to remember that it's not really about you. The magic happens when you bring your community together. It's about the experience, and that experience is heightened when your community members find themselves in a space where they can connect with each other, too.

When April was at her first concert, on one side of her was her best friend, and on the other side was a random girl, probably around the same age. They immediately struck up a conversation with each other

---

[7] For more information about the next FlynnCon, head to FlynnCon.com. I'd love to see you there!

because—guess what? They already had something in common, or else they wouldn't have all been there together. After the opening act (Aaron Carter, Nick Carter's little brother), they had a little time to chat and found out that Nick was their favorite band member! All three of the girls sang and danced all night and had the time of their life.

Gigs are about the community, because community is about other people: you with them, and them with each other. But who is your community, exactly? How do you identify them, and address them as a group? It's about time you brought your active audience even further together by giving them an identity to rally around, and that's what we'll talk about next.

EXERCISE

Stage your first gig. If you've never staged a gig or don't have the resources to create a live, in-person event yet, I recommend starting with something online. You don't have to find a venue, you don't have to go anywhere, and you can get used to showing up and talking in the comfort of your own home.

STEP 1

Decide the platform you'll use for your gig: Facebook Live, Instagram Live, YouTube Live, Periscope, or something else? The easiest way to figure this out is twofold: 1. Which platform are you the most comfortable with, and 2. Where is the majority of your audience already hanging out and engaging with you?

STEP 2

Set a date and time, and announce it to your audience. Do this right away, because as soon as you announce it, you're accountable to your fans to actually show up!

STEP 3

Come up with a short three-point outline for what you will talk about during the live event. Maybe you'll answer three most frequently asked questions, or offer three tips for how to do something related to your niche. Whatever it is, write them down in a place where you can have it for the gig—Post-it Notes are great for this!

STEP 4

Rehearse. Now, don't get me wrong, your live appearance doesn't have to be flawless—it's live, after all, and you want to give your fans a glimpse of what the real you and your real life is like. But it does help to practice a few things: how you start and how you end.

STEP 5

Show up at your planned date and time, go live, and have fun!

LET'S GO DEEPER

In chapter 10 of your *Superfans* Bonus Companion Course, you'll find a number of additional resources for helping you stage your first event, big or small, online or off. Visit **yoursuperfans.com/course**.

CHAPTER 11

GIVE THEM A NAME

On September 8, 1966, the first episode of *Star Trek: The Original Series* aired on NBC, to mixed reviews. *Variety* said "it wouldn't work," and after seeing relatively low numbers during its first season, most thought *Star Trek* was doomed to be cancelled. To everyone's surprise, however, the show began to inspire its own little community of fans.

After just one season, more than 29,000 fan letters arrived in NBC's mailroom, more than any other show in NBC's lineup apart from *The Monkees*. Then, in late 1967, after rumors of cancellation, *Star Trek's* creator, Gene Roddenberry, led and funded a secret campaign to save the program. Using four thousand names on a mailing list for a science fiction convention, Roddenberry's team asked people to write a letter to NBC and find ten friends to do the same.

Between December 1967 and March 1968, over 116,000 letters poured in. Several newspapers wrote columns to help support the campaign, and students from schools like Caltech, MIT, and Berkeley even protested the cancellation, toting signs that said "Draft Spock" and "Vulcan Power."

Then, on March 1, 1968, NBC decided to make a formal announcement on air that they were going to renew the show, a highly unusual move for a network to do. Likely it was because it wanted people to stop writing in, but just as many letters arrived after the announcement thanking NBC for renewing the show. Since then, more and more versions of the show have aired, totaling 31 seasons and over 740 episodes.

When fans get together to support the thing they love, it can be a powerful force that can change the fate of that thing. It was the Trekkies who saved *Star Trek*.

The term *Trekkie* was first used in an interview for *TV Guide* in 1967 by science fiction editor Arthur W. Saha after he'd begun to notice a huge growth in sci-fi interest, and the cult-like fandom of many *Star Trek* viewers in particular. And the name has stuck. To this day, fans of *Star Trek* identify themselves and each other as Trekkies, gathering in the tens of thousands each year at conventions and other events. And they all know that when they get there, there's one thing they're going to see: someone just like them.

A name may seem like a simple thing, but it's really powerful. When you're a member of a community with a name, you have an identity as part of a group that rallies around the brand or artist and is even willing to fight for a common goal. Taylor Swift, for example, has her group of fans called Swifties, consisting of millions of people who not only enjoy her music but also come to her aid when she needs it. Whether it's a disagreement with a record label or platform, gossip in the media, or Kanye West stealing her time on stage, Swifties are there to support their icon like their lives depend on it. The same goes with Justin Bieber and his Beliebers, Lady Gaga and her Little Monsters, Beyonce's Beyhive, and fans of One Direction, The Directioners, who were pretty heartbroken when the group broke up in 2016. You've also got the Potterheads (fans of Harry Potter) and the Twi-hards (fans of the *Twilight* series).

Fan communities with names are not just for TV shows, movies, and music groups. Sports teams name their fans too. Fans of the Oakland Raiders, an American football team, are known as Raider Nation. They even have a section of their stadium known as The Black Hole where their superfans—some of the most notorious fans in all of football because of their pirate-like costumes and crazy energy—congregate. Other football teams, like the Seattle Seahawks and Texas A&M (among others), refer to their fans as The 12th Man. With 11 players on the field at a time, being known as The 12th Man allows fans to feel like they're on the field with the home team, giving the players a competitive advantage.

Now, you might be thinking that naming your community isn't possible because you're not a movie, musician, sports team, or TV show. Not true—you can and very much should give your audience a name! Many YouTubers, for example, have given their fan communities clever monikers. You could try something humorous, like Grace Helbig, an American comedian and YouTuber with three million subscribers who named her community the Gracists. Or something dorky, like the Vlogbrothers, John and Hank Green, who call their fans the Nerdfighters—and they even have an insignia to go along with it. Or there's the straightforward approach, like the one taken by PewDiePie, the most popular YouTuber of all time with more than ninety million subscribers and counting, whose band of devoted followers is named simply the Bros.

Even podcasters are playing the name game. John Lee Dumas, a long-time podcaster and friend of mine who has recorded and published over two thousand interviews with other entrepreneurs on his podcast, *Entrepreneurs on Fire*, has dubbed his community Fire Nation. He even holds meetups at conferences and events that are for Fire Nation only, which brings his community even closer to each other and to the brand itself. One of his most used catch phrases when he's trying to "fire up" his community? *Are you ready to ignite?!*

I didn't name my community until 2018. Before, my fans were simply called the SPI Community, but after learning more about how other people have fostered an identity for their own communities, I decided to give mine a purposeful name. I went for something that would be meaningful in a way that could bring us together, and in this competitive space of entrepreneurship, something that would help us band together for our bigger mission of serving more people. I decided to call my community Team Flynn.

As I always say, we're in this together, on the same team. I may be the team captain, the one with the most experience who you can trust, but sometimes I'm going to pass you the ball and give you a chance to score.

Since adopting Team Flynn into the language I use with my community, I've started getting tons of comments, especially on YouTube, from people who are always thankful for being a part of the team. As many of these commenters say, "Team Flynn for the win!"

I highly recommend giving your community a name. It's a great way to strengthen the identity of your fanbase and give people something to rally around. Sometimes people will come up with a name on their own, but there's a good chance you'll have to be the one to establish a name and use it until it becomes second nature for everyone.

A community that has a name has no excuse not to get together in a close-knit setting! Our next strategy is all about using the humble but oh-so-effective meetup to bring people into the same room, where they can form stronger connections with you and with each other.

EXERCISE

Come up with a name for your community.

STEP 1

Brainstorm a list of five community names. Here are some basic guidelines. The name should:

- Be somewhat catchy and memorable.
- Capture the spirit of you and your brand.
- Embody the community feeling that you want your audience to associate with you and with each other.
- Be original enough to not be confused with other names.

STEP 2

Narrow your list of names to the best one. You could even crowdsource the decision to your audience, a la the Let Them Decide strategy from chapter 7.

STEP 3

Once you've picked a name, use it! Stick with it for a while and you'll begin to see people be associated with it. Hopefully, over time, your people will begin to relate to each other as a member of your named community, too.

STEP 4

Once the name has stuck, consider creating swag or other things that show off the name, like t-shirts, stickers, or tote bags. These things help people feel like they're a part of the community with a shared identity.

STEP 5

If you like, come up with a related phrase or saying to go along with the name, like my "Team Flynn for the Win" or John Lee Dumas's "Are you ready to ignite?" It could sound corny, so think ahead and ask yourself if it's something you really want people saying all the time, because they will.

BRING THEM TOGETHER

During a trip to St. Louis to speak at FinCon13, I rented out a large section of a restaurant and invited one hundred fans to an SPI dinner. Over the course of the night, I shook a lot of hands, gave a lot of hugs, and took a bunch of selfies. It was, as always, an amazing experience to meet my community in person, and I typically use the opportunity to ask a lot of questions, like, "What was your favorite episode of my podcast?" and "If there's something I can do better for you, what would it be?" I try to get to everyone because it gives me a lot I can take home and implement in my business.

At the end of the evening, I noticed a woman who I hadn't yet had a chance to speak to. As everyone was exiting the restaurant, I went up to her and apologized that we hadn't had time to chat, and her response was not what I expected.

"Pat, thank you so much, but please don't take this the wrong way. I didn't come here to see you … "

I was a little stunned, but then she kept going.

"I love you and your work, Pat. I hear you every day on your podcast. But, I never get to meet other entrepreneurs at my level in person. Thank you so much for putting this together and giving me the chance to meet some new friends."

And there you have it. If a gig is about bringing the community together to see you, then a meetup is about bringing the community together for each other.

Every month, I host an entrepreneur meetup in San Diego. It's called the San Diego Entrepreneurs Group, and it started in 2016. We have between thirty and fifty people show up each month, plus an annual bigger event before a conference that happens each year in San Diego. (Those larger meetups have up to four hundred people). It's been amazing to help people feel like they're a part of something, and to feel like they're with *their people*. It's a small commitment, and it's free (hosted at a local WeWork coworking space), but it's actually helped my business. Several people have invited others into the group, and it's a great way for me to stay connected to my audience.

A big reason meetups are so great for building engaged community is that they're versatile. They can be casual, like a dinner or lunch somewhere, or they can be more structured, like a mastermind group. They can even be virtual events coordinated across different locations around the world at the same time. Or, they can be a healthy excuse to indulge in some good old LEGO building.

When it comes to building community through meetups, the Adult Fans of LEGO (AFOL) are a phenomenon to be reckoned with. This worldwide collection of LEGO aficionados is so big that it has its own wiki and subreddit, as well as chapters around the world that host regular real-world meetups. At these meetups, fans get together to take part in collaborative or competitive LEGO building, socialize, and even bid on rare or one-of-a-kind LEGO sets. These LEGO fans get to spend quality time with people similar to them, sharing in the brand and the activity they all love. And the meetups don't require a ton of advanced planning or come with a load of logistical concerns. For AFOLs, these meetups are a fantastic way to blend their love of LEGO with their desire to be part of a community.

And this phenomenon, of people coming together around shared interests, isn't just limited to adults who love to create new worlds with plastic blocks. It's true: today, the meetup *itself* is a phenomenon to be reckoned with. The AFOL gatherings are just one example among many, many successful meetups happening around the world every day across every interest imaginable. As of 2017, the website Meetup.com, probably the most popular destination for organizing real-world meetups online, boasted eight million members in one hundred countries, and more than eighty thousand "Meetup Groups" that collectively scheduled fifty thousand meetups each week.

The meetup is a wonderful and accessible way to build your own engaged community. And no one exemplified the people-gathering power of the meetup better than Scott Dinsmore. Scott had built an amazing tribe over at LiveYourLegend.net, where he and his wife, Chelsea, inspire people all around the world to live their best life. Meetups, known as Live Your Legend LOCAL in their brand, are a huge part of building their community and supporting their mission. As Scott put it:

> "My big lifetime vision for Live Your Legend LOCAL is to have a Live Your Legend Local community within twenty miles of every city and town in the world so no matter where you are, you always have a local support group of inspiring people—in the real world—to help you find and do work that matters."

They recruit local hosts all over the world to help organize these meetups so that the community can have a chance to meet each other, no matter what part of the world they live in. The Live Your Legend community includes more than one hundred sixty thousand people, with over one hundred cities represented.

Scott was a good friend of mine. I met him in person and we shared a few meals together, and his energy radiated in everything he said and did. He was truly on a mission to bring the world together for good. Sadly, while on a hike up Mount Kilimanjaro in 2015, he passed away after being hit by falling rocks near the summit. It took a heavy toll on me and the rest of the blogging community he was a part of, and it was a huge loss for the Living Legends community.

Scott's wife, Chelsea, has continued to foster the community they built together, and even though Scott is not with us here today, his effort to grow a community of Living Legends still lives on. As the Living Your Legend team wrote on the team blog on September 15 after announcing his death, "As we all grapple with this devastating news and heartbreak, we can take some comfort in this amazing community Scott has created. He leaves an incredible legacy of possibility, inspiration, and downright action."

Scott is a legend, and he and his mission live on through the community he built. He represented, as much as anyone I've ever known, what it means to bring people together. He was, in the terminology of author Malcolm Gladwell, a "Connector."

In his book *The Tipping Point*, Gladwell writes about three archetypes of people you tend to find in the world: Mavens, Connectors, and Salespersons. The archetypes differ from each other based on how they make change happen. If you're a Maven, you create change through ideas and information—think engineers, scientists, and other people interested in data and processes. If you're a Connector, you make change happen by connecting people; you're like a "hub" for others to network. And if you're a Salesperson, you make change happen through persuasion; you know how to tell stories and convince people to think or act a certain way.

Does one of those archetypes describe you? There's a good chance you align with one more than the others. But here's the thing: even if you consider yourself more of a Maven or Salesperson, I want to challenge you to unlock your inner Connector, because that's what's going to help you succeed with this strategy of bringing people together.

But how do you do that if it doesn't come naturally to you? In *The Tipping Point*, Gladwell tells the story of a woman named Lois Weisberg who was a natural Connector:

> "Weisberg, one of her friends told me, 'always says— "Oh, I've met the most wonderful person. You are going to love her," and she is as enthused about this person as she was about the first person she has met and you know what, she's usually right.' Helen Doria, another of her friends, told me that 'Lois sees things in you that you don't even see in yourself,' which is another way of saying the same thing, that by some marvelous quirk

of nature, Lois and the other people like her have some instinct that helps them relate to the people they meet."[8]

Gladwell goes on to say that when a Connector "looks out at the world . . . they don't see the same world that the rest of us see. They see possibility . . . " Connectors like Lois see value in every person they meet. They *like* everybody for who they are. They find real potential in everyone they encounter.

If you want to build a brand and a community that's rich with engagement, then you have to tap into your inner Connector, however small that part of you may be. Even if you don't feel like you have the connecting instinct Gladwell describes, you can still make a conscious decision to seek out the interesting aspects in everyone you meet, to welcome people into the fold and invite them to share all of their unique contributions and insights with you and your community.

Even if a Connector mentality isn't a huge part of who you are, the beauty is that once you start to tap into that small piece of yourself and put it into action, you'll set in motion something much bigger than you, something with its own momentum. People will take the energy of connection they experience at your meetups and channel it outward in exciting ways. At my meetups, not only are people there to connect with each other, but they form friendships, partnerships, and even their own meetups and mastermind groups to make the magic happen in an even wider circle.

A few people have told me about the community connection they experience through the SPI meetups, like Diane and Kacie. Diane says attending her first meetup made her want to keep engaging with the community, and Kacie joined the SPI Facebook group after her first meetup. She even says that she now pays closer attention to my emails.

Ongoing meetups provide even greater value for regular attendees like Wendy, who told me that she knows the group is a place to continue learning and growing, where she can reach out for information or

---

[8] Malcolm Gladwell, *The Tipping Point: How Little Things Can Make a Big Difference*, (Little, Brown, 2000), 53.

resources. She even made a powerful connection with someone she met two years ago, and now they are accountability partners.

You've given your community a name, and gotten the hang of creating gigs and meetups to bring people together. Now let's focus on bringing your active audience members to the forefront, where you can celebrate their unique abilities, accomplishments, and ambitions, and help make them and the rest of your audience even more engaged members of the community!

EXERCISE

Create your first meetup!

STEP 1

Pick a date and a venue, and have an idea of roughly how many people you'd like to show up at that space. Your meetup doesn't have to be super formal. It can be as simple as meeting at a local coffee shop or at a park. And as far as size, I've hosted meetups back in the day with only three or four people, and they were awesome!

STEP 2

Set up the meetup on meetup.com or eventbrite.com.

STEP 3

Let your audience know about it! Not everyone will be able to make it because of the time and location, and that's okay. The truth is, however, no one will show up unless you let them know when and where it'll be, so get out of your comfort zone and share it!

STEP 4

Show up (bring name tags and markers if you'd like) and enjoy having and hosting the conversations!

CHAPTER 13

MAKE THEM SHINE

Being half Filipino on my mom's side, I've had a lifelong immersion in Filipino culture. Foods like lumpia, pancit, and chicken adobo over rice were a staple growing up. Large potluck gatherings for any occasion were normal, and so was the karaoke sung at those parties. But if there's one thing I've learned about being Filipino and around a lot of Filipinos growing up, it's that we are a very proud people—so proud that anytime a Filipino person gets a little positive spotlight in the media, the entire nation gets behind them.

During season three of *American Idol*, Filipino–American Jasmine Trias, born in Honolulu, Hawaii, and the eldest daughter of Filipino immigrants, became a household name. My mom and all of the other Filipino parents in the community couldn't stop talking about her and the songs she sang each week, sometimes analyzing them to the point you'd think they were her singing coaches. We'd rally each other to dial in and vote to keep sending Jasmine through to the next round, and we felt a sense of pride every time she made it through. She got to the top three.

Manny Pacquiao is another Filipino sensation, one of the greatest pound-for-pound boxers of all time. Every time he fought, the entire Filipino community would stop everything and be glued to their televisions.

In the Philippines, stores closed and the streets were empty, because everyone was watching, rooting for their fighter and their country to win. Even people who weren't really into boxing were mesmerized because of who Manny represented. When he won, we all won. And when he lost, we'd all feel the defeat.

It's similar to the Olympics. Most people don't participate in track and field or swimming or ice hockey, and most of us don't personally know anyone participating in these events. But when it comes time to compete, we stand behind our country and the people who represent it. We get emotional at times, crying in agony when we just miss the gold, or shouting with a huge sense of pride when we win. We love seeing people in our community do well. It inspires and moves us.

That's why if you have a community, you should be going out of your way to feature your community members.

A couple years ago, my son Keoni was a huge Minecraft fan. One of his favorite YouTubers was a massively popular Minecraft player who goes by the nickname Stampy Cat (as well as Stampylongnose and Stampylonghead), who today has amassed more than nine million subscribers, published books, and even created plush toys that represent his avatar in the Minecraft world. In several of his videos (Keoni watched a few a day) he would give a shoutout to some of his fans, even featuring their names on a little digital sign in a part of his Minecraft world which he called his "Love Garden." Fans would create artwork for him, then he'd share it with the rest of his audience, commenting on it and sharing the person's name. I'm sure it made them feel amazing!

I'm willing to bet you've been to at least one sporting event (or seen one on TV) where during timeouts, the camera zooms in on people in the crowd and projects them on a huge screen in the middle of the venue. And I'm willing to bet you've noticed that most of the time, people relish this attention. They'll start screaming and pointing at themselves up on the screen, high-fiving their seatmates. If there's music playing, they'll start dancing (or if they're already dancing, they'll kick up their moves a notch or three). In general, people love to be highlighted, especially if they're with a group of like-minded people who are sharing and enjoying the same experience. And this can work to your advantage whether you're the owner of an NBA team or a solo entrepreneur trying to build your small online community into something great.

Every once in a while, highlight some of the amazing things your community members are doing. At this point in the journey, especially after communicating with your audience and seeing how they communicate with each other, there are likely some standout people you can highlight and bring to the surface for everyone to see. This has worked really well in the SPI community, because it shows people that others just like them can build a business from scratch and succeed. Sometimes, your community members can even do a better job of getting your people to move than you can.

One of the coolest retail communities I've seen is the one associated with a brand called Chubbies. Chubbies makes men's shorts, and the brand's ideal customer persona is the weekender who enjoys barbecues and parties by the lake on a hot weekend. After interviewing the founder of Chubbies, Tom Montgomery, on *SPI Podcast* episode 269, I learned that they'd built a huge fan base, one of the most devoted I've seen in the retail space, and one that goes crazy whenever new products are promoted. But it was how they built this fanbase that was the most fascinating. Chubbies grew this devoted community using the simple tactic of featuring their community members. In the interview, Tom explains:

> "In the world of Instagram, one of the things that we saw from day one is that when people got the product, they started sending us photos. It was amazing, and they're just the most diverse, ridiculous group of people. That's the fuel for our Instagram feed. So if you look at our Instagram feed, for 95 percent of all the posts in there, those are customers."

Chubbies took this idea of featuring the community to a whole new level in 2015:

> "Whether it was through email or Instagram, we always wanted to showcase the community. We took that kind of to its furthest extent where in 2015, we hired male

models out of our community of customers and people who were fans of the brand. Those are the models that we use."

In my business, I try to do something similar on a regular basis—okay, not the male models part, but showcasing community members. The podcast is a great place to feature the SPI community, and sometimes we invite people on the show to share their success stories. If you have customers, showcase them in some way using your product. But don't make it about your product—make it about their experience: where they were before, and where they are now. Show examples of things that have happened to them since using your product. Instead of you selling your product, your customers will do it for you, but in a natural, organic, nonaggressive way.

On *SPI Podcast* episode 275, for example, I interviewed three students of one of my courses, Power-Up Podcasting. I timed the episode to go live the same week I launched Power-Up Podcasting, and it was a major contributing factor to the course's six-figure launch. I know this because of the tracking coming from the links mentioned in the show, as well as the sheer number of emails and messages from people telling me it was *that* podcast episode and the stories they heard that convinced them to purchase my course.

When doing this, it's always great to feature a range of different people from your audience. This way, it's more likely that a person reading, listening, or watching will find someone just like them. In episode 275, for example, I brought on Dr. B., host of the *Harness Your ADHD Power Podcast*, who started her show at the age of sixty. She told an amazing story about a map she has pinned to the wall above her computer. Whenever she gets a new listener from a country previously unrepresented in her audience, she puts a pin on the map. At the time of the interview, her show had listeners in over thirty countries, and knowing that she's helping people with ADHD (and those who support others with ADHD) all over the world inspires her to keep going with her podcast.

I also interviewed Dr. Shannon Irvine, a neuropsychologist who told me she was able to use her new podcast to take her existing offline business online and gain new clients. That show, *Epic Success Podcast*, has become the primary lead generator for her business. And finally, I also featured Rob from *Disney Travel Secrets*, who along with his wife, Kerri, used their podcast to grow their Disney travel agency by 348 percent.

I've interviewed more than three hundred people for the *SPI Podcast*, many of whom are considered A-listers at the top of the entrepreneurial industry. But as I mentioned in chapter 4, it's often the episodes with listeners of the show who are a part of the community that get more people to engage. In that chapter I told you how the podcast episode featuring Shane and Jocelyn Sams, two teachers from Kentucky, became a fan favorite in the lineup that's been downloaded more times than a lot of episodes featuring "bigger" names.

There's also Melissa Monte, a student of my Power-Up Podcasting Fast Track Workshop, who joined me on *SPI Podcast* episode 318. We talked about how she created and launched her podcast, *Mind Love*, soon after finishing up the workshop, and what she learned in the process. She even shared personal details about the darker years of her life, and how she was able to overcome them and create a whole new perspective. We talked about why she decided to launch a podcast, and why podcasting is helping her fulfill her life's mission. With her own growing audience, I also offered her advice to help take things to the next level.

Without fail, whenever I feature audience members like Melissa, Rob and Kerri, Shannon, Dr. B., or the Samses on the podcast, the response from the community is awesome. Blog comments are filled with responses from people who are inspired by these people's stories. Check out some of the comments that came in for *SPI Podcast* episode 195, featuring Carrie Clark, a speech therapist by trade who built her website, SpeechandLanguageKids.com, into an amazing passive income success story through smart monetization, community building, and a successful membership program:

> "As a fellow Speech-Language Pathologist and entrepreneur, Carrie's story is especially interesting! I am proud of her drive and success—both for her patients and herself. Congratulations, Carrie. Keep up the good work!"

"I loved this episode. Carrie you really are an inspiration—as you are Pat. I'm a few steps behind you in the curve of building up the business, but working on something similar in the music education space. I too love working with preschoolers! Congrats!"

"Hey Carrie, congrats! You're such an inspiration, and $10k a month is my goal too."

"Thank you for this podcast!!! I'm a pediatric OT and just quit my job at Primary Children's Hospital because I can't see myself spending thirty more years with the limitations and frustrations of the current healthcare environment."

"I was super inspired by this podcast! Carrie, I can totally relate to your path. I'm a financial wellness coach focusing on one-on-one coaching, while trying to expand my platform on the side. Your story validates this as a viable path. I love how you persevered. It gives me hope when I'm tempted to feel discouraged at results."

There's a reason stories like these, featuring down to earth folks who have gone on to do awesome things, resonate so much with my audience. The people telling these stories are more relatable, and that's why featuring community members is so important: It's social proof in action. When people see others like them succeeding using the ideas you teach, they're more likely to see themselves and their own potential in a similar light. And they're going to want to stick around and engage.

If you want your audience to stay engaged, you need to bring them on the court and pass them the ball. Give your people a chance to shine, and to feel like they belong. Or to use another metaphor, you've built this wonderful stage, so it's time to share it. In early 2018, famous rock band the Foo Fighters was playing a concert in Brisbane, Australia. As the show was winding to a close, a fan named Joey McClennan stood in the audience holding a sign he'd made the night before asking the band: *Can I play "Monkey Wrench?"* His unlikely wish came true when lead singer Dave Grohl invited Joey onstage, handed him a guitar, asked him, "Are you sure you can play it?" (a fact Joey eagerly confirmed), then proceeded to let Joey live out his dream shredding with his favorite band in front of thousands of other fans.

Naturally, Joey's rock star moment hit social media big time, and thousands of commenters on YouTube were wowed by the simple but incredible opportunity of playing guitar onstage with their musical heroes.[9] Joey's cameo even sparked a mini-trend for the Foo Fighters, who invited fans onstage to play guitar with them at several more of their shows in 2018, like ten-year-old Collier Rule, who jammed with the band in Kansas City and got to walk offstage with Dave Grohl's guitar in his hands and stars in his eyes.

You don't have to be a rock star to pull off this strategy, of course. You just have to open the stage to the people who want to share it with you. Our final strategy of part two is similar to this one, but it's all about zeroing in on the members of your audience who are the most active and ready to become catalysts for engagement.

---

[9] Luke Sorensen, "BEST VERSION - FOO FIGHTERS Brisbane 2018 fan on stage Joey McClennan plays Monkey Wrench," (Jan 31, 2018), https://www.youtube.com/watch?v=nBYSDnsVGv4

EXERCISE

Find a way to feature your community members.

STEP 1

Generate a list of all the possible ways you can feature people from your community: blog posts, podcast interviews, video interviews, social media posts, email newsletter, etc.

___

STEP 2

Generate a feature type for each medium on your list. For example, is the blog post Q&A style, a guest post, or a narrative write-up about the person?

___

STEP 3

Choose one idea to implement, and plan to do it consistently for a set amount of time to gauge reaction and success of the strategy. Keep the other ideas in your backlog for use in the future.

___

STEP 4

If and when it makes sense, look for other bigger opportunities like creating an award and presenting it to someone for "community member of the year," or another achievement that aligns with your brand and deserves recognition. Bonus: this could even be done in person from stage if you eventually host a live event for your fans.

This is one of the most special phases of building your superfan journey, because you're not just developing individual fans, but bringing together your community to rally around your brand and each other.

You're creating fan-building experiences, building those magical moments for your active audience and also giving them a way to create those moments for one another. Think about fans in an arena after their team has won the big game. They all celebrate together, high-fiving and maybe even hugging and kissing people they've never even met. This kind of bond can't happen unless they have a powerful reason to be together in that place and at that time: their team.

When you give people something to root for, you give them a reason to stay connected. So be the team that brings people together.

Open up your brand and your business to your audience. Ask them questions, and give them a forum to share their answers. Allow them to have a hand in the decisions you make in your business. Challenge them to reach their own goals, and to support each other along the way. Let them backstage so they can see how the magic happens and learn from your processes. Then, bring them together in bigger ways. Create your own gigs and meetups, events where you can talk to your audience and they can connect with each other in intimate and powerful ways. Finally, let your community members take their place on stage with you to share their stories, whether it's featuring them in your podcast, thanking them publicly on your Facebook page, or yes, literally bringing them up on stage at one of your events.

Oh, and don't forget to give your community a cool name.

In the next phase of our journey together, you'll learn four more strategies to complete your audience's path to becoming superfans—the secret button combination to press on the elevator of fandom, one that will delightfully whisk the most engaged members of your community right to the top of the pyramid.

PART 3

CONNECTED COMMUNITY TO SUPERFANS

B y following the strategies laid out in the book so far, you're going to develop some raving superfans, even without any extra effort. But there are a few more strategies we need to cover, ones that exist on a level higher than the "one to many" strategies we've tackled so far. These personalized actions will help put the dedicated fans in your audience over the top and into the super *stratum* of fandom.

I met an older couple at a hotel bar on a business trip once, and it was one of the most important and memorable encounters I've ever had. Their names were Jean and Ted, and they were celebrating their fiftieth wedding anniversary. You could tell they were still deeply in love with each other. It made my heart melt.

I noticed a nearly empty bottle of chardonnay between them and offered to buy them another as a gift to celebrate. Although they said no at first, after I mentioned I'd be happy to share it with them, they agreed. Since I was the one who'd ordered it, the bartender presented me with the first sip and the cork, but I wasn't interested in the wine. I wanted to learn more about Jean and Ted and how they'd been able to stay together for so long. As a married man myself, I always look for inspiration and opportunities to learn how to become a better husband, and who better to survey than a couple celebrating their fiftieth wedding anniversary together, at a bar, giggling like kids on a playground.

After a few sips, I eventually asked them: "You've been married for fifty years. What's your secret? How did you do it?"

They laughed and looked at each other, confirming that I was not the first person to ask them that question that day. But, they were quick to jump into a response. Jean started with a quick backstory about how she and Ted met in high school, which involved her declining Tom's prom proposal but then going with him anyway and having a blast. They started dating after that and went to the same local college, where Tom proposed to her during their senior year.

At this point, Tom quickly stepped in and added: "And do you know how I did it? I got down on one knee, showed her the ring, and I asked her to prom again!"

He laughed so loud it seemed like the entire bar looked at us, and they probably saw me smiling ear to ear, because it was an awesome story.

After the laughter died down, Jean leaned toward me and said, "Pat, here's why we've been able to stay together for so long. It's because in addition to the morning coffee we have together each day, and the good-night kiss each night before bed, our days are filled with random acts of kindness toward each other, little things, nothing big usually, that remind us we're worth breaking routine for."

Interrupting the pattern. This is huge and makes perfect sense, because those random things are the things that get remembered. Routines are great, don't get me wrong. They help us build healthy habits and allow us to automate a lot of our day, but when it comes to people, automation can only take you so far. It's the thoughtful, unautomated moments that can take you to the next level.

Ted then told a story about something he did as an example, when they were in their early forties.

"Pat, you're gonna love this," he said. (I love how he already knew this.) "One day, I was at work and Jean called me at lunch to check in. She mentioned she forgot her reading glasses at home. I didn't tell her, but I went straight home, grabbed her glasses, and then dropped them off at her office. I also wrote a little note. On one side I wrote, 'You'll need these glasses to read this note,' and on the other side I wrote, 'I love you.' The secretary gave it to her, and boy, you know I got some good cooking that night!"

Jean added, "And I didn't even *need* the glasses. The day was almost over, and that's what made it even more special. And the ladies in the office, I'll tell you," as she looked over at Ted, "they were saying things like, 'I wish my husband did that kind of thing, or 'I need a man like that.'"

I heard a lot more stories from Jean and Ted and got to tell a few of my own, but after about an hour they were met by a family friend and had to leave. So we said our goodbyes and I offered one more "happy anniversary" for the road. It was a wonderful time that I'll remember and cherish forever, and I immediately texted my wife after to tell her I loved her.

Whether you're into sappy love stories or not (and yes, this one is true), you can't deny the fact that Jean and Ted's advice was spot on: In order to become someone's ultimate favorite, you have to do the things other people aren't going to do. You have to be more than different, because different got you in the door—you have to remain thoughtful. It's the random, unexpected acts of kindness, no matter how big or small, that will help you be not only remembered, but like with Jean's coworkers, also talked about and shared.

This part of the book is all about the powerful personal things you can do to make a big impact, and hopefully get your community to understand why they should be superfans, and also to share their love for your community with others.

Making things irregular and unexpected is the key thing here—your audience will get used to a pattern. Break that pattern and help them remember why they love you, and why you should always be in their life. And most importantly, give without asking for anything in return.

This part of the book will focus on the unforgettable moments and experiences you'll be creating to break the seal and create superfans for life. We're going to be building on some of the ideas from part two in particular, but adding an individualized touch, one that's going to make your fans feel like heroes. Everyone loves a good hero story, and when you can create ways for your audience to become the hero, they're going to stick with you for life.

Here's what we'll cover in this section:

- ▶ **CHAPTER 14: REMEMBER THE LEMONS**
- ▶ **CHAPTER 15: SEND UNEXPECTED MESSAGES**
- ▶ **CHAPTER 16: GET THEM INVOLVED**
- ▶ **CHAPTER 17: OFFER PLATINUM ACCESS**

All right. Let's go get you some superfans.

REMEMBER THE LEMONS

W hen I was in college at UC Berkeley, I made a little extra money by waiting tables at a local Macaroni Grill. It wasn't the finest Italian cuisine, but I enjoyed the food and had some friends who were already working at the same restaurant, so it was pretty cool. Just for fun, when my friends and I were all working the same shift, we played a little game with each other: whoever could make the most tips during the shift would collect $10 from each of the other players. With three of us playing at first, and then a few more coworkers jumping in, we sometimes had up to six people playing. If you won, you could make an extra $50! The energy was high, and I was determined to learn all the tricks to getting the most tips possible, every single time.

I picked up some good tricks, too. For example, whenever a family with kids came in, I learned that if I focused on making sure the kids were happy, I'd generally see a much larger tip. As a parent now, I completely understand: All a parent wants to do when eating out is have an event-free, tantrum-free meal, and that applies to all ages between zero and eighteen. Anyone who helps you make sure that happens is worth a little extra.

If an elementary school kid was at the table, it was easy: crayons. Specifically, red and blue. I kept a handful of red and blue crayons in my pocket so that in addition to the two random colors on the table, I could swing back around after taking the family's order and pop a couple more crayons on the table for the kid. Why red and blue? Because those are typically kids' favorite colors. Plus you can draw more things, like the sky and ocean, and hearts and flowers. If there were two or more kids at the table, I always made sure each kid had the exact same colors, no more, no less. Why? Because all it takes is one difference for a child to complain. Sharing is encouraged, but in a situation like this, two of the same thing makes sense.

There was good money here, but the best money came from (drum roll, please …) regulars. Over a few months of waiting on some of the customers who made the restaurant part of their schedule, it became obvious that this was where the money could be made. Let me tell you about Albert and the three lemons.

Albert was a middle-aged businessman who often came in late in the evenings each week, in business attire, with a colleague or two. They had paperwork and seemed to discuss really important things, which was a sign for me to keep the chatter to a minimum. (That's another tactic I used to get more tips: be just like your customer. If they talk to you a lot, talk to them a lot. If they're short with words, then don't talk more than you have to.)

I didn't wait on Albert the first few times I saw him come in, but when I finally had a chance to wait on him, I looked for ways I could make his life even easier. First, I paid attention to his order. If it was the same the next time, then I could assume it would be "his usual." Are there any special requests? Pay attention to those, too. I noticed that with his water, he asked for three lemons. Not some or a bunch, but three. Duly noted.

When getting that check back from his table the first time, his tip was pretty standard: $10 on a $60–$70 check. About 15 percent. But that check also told me something even more important: his name. The next time he came in, I was going to make sure Albert knew he was remembered and that he felt special.

The next time Albert walked in, I sat him and his colleague down and said I'd be right back to take their order. On my way back, I brought two waters and a little dish with three lemons on it for Albert. Then, remembering his name, I asked him in this manner, "Albert, what can I get for you tonight?" I didn't do my usual spiel about the specials or wine, I just made it quick, and he was quick to answer: Carmela's Chicken Rigatoni—again. Then, I followed up with, "Shall I call this your usual from now on, sir?" Then he paused, looked at me and said, "That would be fantastic!"

I made sure to seal the deal. "Just ask for Pat each time you come in. I'll take care of you and your colleagues."

Boom. It was a done deal. Every single time Albert came in, which was usually once a week, I served him when I was there. When I wasn't there, my coworkers would tell me that he asked for me. Now, if you're wondering how this kind of attention played a role in the size of his tips, then you're like most people. Unfortunately, this is what gets most people in trouble.

Of course you're wondering—I set up this whole chapter to be about the tip size—but the truth is, the tip size is a result of the service, and your earnings are a byproduct of how well you serve. When you go above and beyond to serve someone, you will be rewarded—sometimes in money, sometimes in exposure or referrals, and sometimes just with a thank you, but the universe has this amazing way of giving back to those who serve first. Let the money come from extraordinary service.

Yes, Albert's tips were significantly higher. Not right away, but over time, the tips started ranging from $20–$25, with the largest being $100 when he brought his whole office in one day. And yes, each time Albert came in, my coworkers knew that I was probably going to be a front runner for our little game that day.

Serve first, pay attention to the individual, and you will be rewarded.

Now, you can't just go and give three lemons to every person you wait on. That'd be a waste of lemons, and you wouldn't be listening to the customer. Not all customers, audiences, subscribers, and followers are the same, but if you want someone to know you're there for them, make them stick around and become a true, lifelong superfan by paying close attention to what they need and what you can do for them.

Now, can you possibly deliver individualized service to every fan in your audience? Again, probably not—but the three lemons example still gives us some hints about how to succeed. It's as simple as remembering who people are and making your interactions with them about *them*, not you.

In fact, you can make a huge difference just by remembering someone's name. As Dale Carnegie said in *How to Win Friends and Influence People*, "Remember that a person's name is to that person the sweetest and most important sound in any language."[10] Greeting someone using their name—especially if they don't expect you to—is a powerful signal that you're interested in them as more than just another member of your audience. But you can and should go beyond simply remembering and using someone's name. Remember other details of their lives: their business, their family, their hobbies. Then show curiosity—ask them about these things! They'll be delighted.

I love to put this strategy into action when I attend live events. When I'm at a conference, I always make sure to look out for people in my audience I recognize, whether it's folks who've bought my courses, active members of the Facebook community, or people I've talked to over email.

When I'm chatting with these fans, I make sure to show curiosity about them and what they're working on. Often, people are pleasantly surprised when I show genuine interest in who they are and how their business is going. There's a person in my audience named Tyler who's purchased a lot of my courses. He's been an engaged and supportive member of the SPI community for quite some time. I've even had several conversations with him via direct message where I've come to know a little bit about his family. When I met Tyler in person for the first time, we quickly launched into the kind of conversation you'd have with a longtime friend.

That's the thing about the three lemons strategy: It's not about the lemons. It's about the fact you *remembered* the lemons. That you cared enough to consider what matters to the diner you're serving, or the fan you're talking to at a conference.

---

[10] Dale Carnegie, *How to Win Friends and Influence People*, 79.

Be human. Be curious about people. Show that you're excited to see them, and that you care about their needs and interests and the details of their lives. They'll notice, and they'll love it. Up next, the days of "You've got mail!" and the excitement we used to feel when we got a new email in our inbox may be long over, but there's another type of messaging you can use in combination with the Remember the Lemons strategy to surprise and delight your dedicated fans and groom them into superfans.

EXERCISE

Spend time learning about the members of your connected community, then put that knowledge into action at your next event. This works for both offline and online events.

STEP 1

If there are folks who interact with you regularly, follow them back. These are people who reply to your emails, leave comments on your posts, or show up to your live streams. You should start recognizing names and faces.

STEP 2

Scroll through these folks' profiles. What are they frequently posting about? Their kids? Pets? Food? A particular type of food? The house remodel or yard project? The craft hobby? You get the idea: Notice the things these fans are into.

STEP 3

Next time you see these folks engage with you in some way, via a comment on your post or showing up to your live stream, ask them about something specific you remember seeing on their profile. You'll be amazed at the reaction when they realize you're actually noticing them.

CHAPTER 15

SEND UNEXPECTED MESSAGES

"Bonjoro."

"What?" I asked. "Isn't it 'bonjour,' like B-O-N-J-O-U-R?"

"No, it's Bonjoro. B-O-N-J-O-R-O dot com."

I was on the phone with Nathan Barry, founder of ConvertKit, which is an email service platform built to help creators earn a living on-line. Nathan was filling me in on a new tool he and his team were using to onboard new customers. Here's how he described it:

"When a new customer signs up, the Bonjoro app will notify you. You swipe to open a video recording screen where you can record a quick little thank-you video and send it to them immediately. You have their name so you can personalize it, too."

Matt Ragland was a member of Nathan's team. As a product analyst at ConvertKit, Matt was the one who manages the Bonjoro app for the company. Some time after my chat with Nathan, I connected with Matt to understand how he and the team use this tool, and more importantly how it has affected business, if at all.

Matt told me that he spent two to three hours of his workday (at least around the time we talked) walking around, sending video messages. He said, "It's pretty awesome to just show that you're out and about but you still take the time to send a personalized message. And just imagine: you sign up for an email service provider—not the most personal of tools—and get a personalized message from someone who works there and even says your name, thanks you, and welcomes you to the Convert-Kit family." He also described how roughly half the people reply back via email saying it was a pleasant surprise. What a great first impression!

Then, he said something that surprised me. Since implementing Bonjoro to their onboarding workflow, after nine months, user churn had dropped by more than 12 percent. What's churn? It's the rate at which people stop using a paid service. When you're selling a product that requires a monthly or annual payment, you're relying on that ongoing income, so it's important to look at churn and see what you can do to reduce it. The fact that ConvertKit's churn rate had reduced so significantly in so little time just by creating welcome videos for new customers was amazing!

ConvertKit's success with Bonjoro began to open my eyes to the power of small, short, unexpected, personalized messages.

There are different ways to do this—you could send an email, or a direct message on Twitter or Instagram. But if you really want to make an impression and bring out someone's inner superfan, send a video message. Videos, maybe more than any other kind of digital communication, are personal. They suggest more time and effort went into producing and sending them, and since there's a real person with a voice and a face on the other end engaging with you and you alone, it can make a very powerful impression.

After I learned how ConvertKit was using Bonjoro to welcome their new users, I began to wonder how I might be able to use videos like this in my own business to surprise and delight my customers and fans.

I quickly downloaded Bonjoro and immediately started using it in conjunction with the sale of one of my courses. As soon as I started to see the notifications from Bonjoro, no matter where I was, I'd swipe, hit record, and send a quick thank-you video with some initial instructions for how to proceed with the course.

And the response? Wow! More than 80 percent of my customers replied saying how impressed they were, and how they knew they had spent their money in the right place. It validated Matt's perspective, and I was excited to see what else I could do.

Luckily, we live in an age now where small, quick videos are easy to create. Whether you use a sophisticated tool like Bonjoro (which is actually very easy to set up), or create videos on Instagram or Twitter to send to people, a small time investment can go a long way in brightening someone's day and interrupting the pattern of impersonalized media they're used to consuming throughout the day on social media, podcasts, YouTube, and elsewhere.

I took this a step further once I realized just how powerful these small, unexpected video messages could be. I decided to do a little experiment and send personalized videos to fifty people in my audience who I knew had been fans for a while. Some were customers, some were very active people in my community, and others were friends and entrepreneurs I just hadn't heard from in a while. Using Bonjoro to input each name and email individually, I sent a personalized video through the app.

It was the Remember the Lemons strategy combined with the power of the individual message. All in all, it took about two hours to complete.

The next day, I woke up to a barrage of email replies to my videos. Here are a few of them:

> "Pat!! THIS is why I love you, man. Thanks for the video and I hope you and the family are doing well."

> "What a surprise my friend! My friend! Pat! Just wanted to say I loved your last blog post. Huge fan already, and you've just proven why."

> "Pat! You're so generous! Thank you for taking the time to send me a video you really didn't have to do that. It reminded that I owe you a review for your podcast, I'll make sure to get that done today!"

> "Dude. This. This video right here. It's exactly what I needed today. Thank you for keeping me in mind, man. You have no idea how much I needed that. Thank you!"

"You're on another level Pat! Looking forward to the next episode!"

Realize that this isn't anything innovative. Anyone can send anyone a video for any reason—but it's not a strategy a lot of people and brands are putting to good use yet, so the novelty factor is still high. Video still offers the opportunity to stand out from the crowd.

You might be thinking at this point, *What about live streaming?* Live streaming is great, but it's not the one-to-one personal touch we're going for here. Live streaming is great for community building, but it's the fact that you're taking time—even a little bit of time—to think about the individual that makes all the difference in turning community members into superfans.

When email came on the scene in the early nineties, it was fun and exciting to get an email—because there weren't that many to go around. If you were born in the eighties like me, you might remember the early days of America Online (AOL). Every time you got an email, which wasn't very often, you'd hear a man's voice say enthusiastically, "You've got mail!" It was always so exciting to learn someone had sent you something!

Imagine the same thing today: a voice that lets you know when you've got a new email in your inbox. Every. Single. Time. You'd be scrambling to turn off that setting as quickly as possible.

But that's the beauty of video: it has the novelty element. It's not annoying! Video messages are to 2019 what email was to 1995. By sending a video message, you're making it personal and more likely a person is going to a) open that video, b) receive your message, and c) feel the need to respond positively because you've done something unusually thoughtful for them. And that's the keyword: *unusual.*

So how often should you do this, and who should you send videos to? It's really up to you, but plan to make video messages a part of your strategy. If you'd like, use a tool like Bonjoro to automate as much as you can so all you have to worry about is sending the videos. You can send them to new customers, and even new email subscribers. And of course, sending videos to individuals, if you know their email addresses, is easy to do. If a fan speaks up and shares your stuff on social media, take thirty seconds to fire up a video through the social media platform thanking them for being awesome. Do it in your way, your style, so that more of you gets through to that person.

There are other ways to use small, unexpected videos to connect to your audience. Another easy way is with Instagram direct messages. When a person sends me a message or has a question on Instagram, I'll often send a quick video reply. It goes a long way, and people really appreciate it. I'll even go above and beyond sometimes and actually reach out to someone who leaves a positive comment on one of my posts, thanking them for the comment. I don't do this very often, but when I do, it definitely gets a big, positive response. I've also used videos to reply to questions that come in via email and on Twitter.

Think of the short, personalized video message as an alternative to an email reply or direct message, but with way more value and human connection. As I mentioned back in chapter 1, I also like to connect with ten of my new email subscribers each month. I'll reach out to them and ask them to get on a fifteen-minute Skype call. And that's really cool because it gives me a chance to talk one-on-one with someone who may be new to my brand and could have fresh ideas to share. Plus, it's even better when we get to talk live and see each other's face. And video makes that happen.

Individualized video messages are an awesome and easy way to personalize and humanize your interactions with your connected community and give them even more than they expect from you. Going above and beyond like this is a huge key to making people into superfans. In the next chapter, we'll cover another strategy for turning members of your connected community into superfans, which involves making people part of the fabric of the brand and the machinery of your business.

EXERCISE

Practice sending short, personalized messages to your followers.

STEP 1

Similar to the Remember the Lemons strategy, take note of the folks who are engaging and connecting with you on a regular basis.

STEP 2

The next time you see a regular leave a comment or respond to an email, craft a short message—video is great!—letting them know how much you appreciate them. It doesn't have to be more than thirty seconds.

STEP 3

Send the video via the same platform where the interaction happened. If they responded to an email, email them back with a link to a video. If they commented on Instagram, send them a video via DM. (Did you even know you could do this on Instagram? You can!)

CHAPTER 16

GET THEM INVOLVED

There are a few TV shows that stand out above the rest for the level of cult-like fandom they inspire. *Star Trek*, which we talked about in chapter 11, with its devoted Trekkies, is one of them. Another is *Doctor Who*, the British science fiction show about a human-looking alien who explores the universe in a time-traveling spaceship called the TARDIS. After its original run from 1963 to 1989, the show was rebooted in 2005 and has been going strong since. Several decades and nearly nine hundred episodes in, *Doctor Who* is one of the most beloved shows of all time.

In the span of its existence, the Doctor has been played by thirteen different actors. A big part of the show's charm and identity is wrapped up in the many faces of its title character, and the speculation and excitement among the fanbase whenever it's time for the current Doctor to hand over the reins.

In 1972, Peter Capaldi was a fourteen-year-old growing up in Glasgow, Scotland. He was also a huge—and I mean huge—*Doctor Who* fan. He would write in regularly to newspapers expressing his love for the show. He also became infamous for the amount of fan mail he sent to the official *Doctor Who* fan club. In one letter he wrote that year, he even asked that he be made president of the club, but the position was sadly already taken. It would take several more decades, but Capaldi eventually got the best consolation prize he could have asked. In 2013, with the incumbent Doctor, Matt Smith, retiring from the role, Capaldi was announced as the twelfth incarnation of *Doctor Who*, a role he would hold until the beginning of 2017.

It's hard to think of a more perfect fit as the lead actor in a TV show than someone who grew up living and breathing that show. And in a similar way, it's hard to think of a better fit for the people who contribute regularly to your team than those who live and breathe your brand.

In part 2, we talked about ways you can get your community members involved in your brand. By giving them even a little bit of a say—a little bit of ownership in your brand and the direction your brand takes—your community is more likely to support you and your business because they've invested their time, thought, and energy into it. Getting your community directly involved in your brand is a powerful strategy, and yes, these powers can be used both for good and for evil. We'll go over the traps that you could fall into while building a tribe of superfans in the last part of the book, but for now, let's take the idea of community involvement to the next level and talk about how to convert more of those fans into superfans by getting them super involved—as a part of your team.

Not too long ago, April and the kids and I watched a special on Hulu about how the employees at Disneyland decorated the entire park overnight for Halloween. It was remarkable how many of the employees featured were Disney superfans, many of them for almost their entire lives. Disney is part of who they are. There was Antonio Beach, a scenic painter whose grandmother took him to Disneyland when he was just a few years old, and who'd wanted to paint and decorate at Disneyland since he was ten. At the age of twenty-two, finally working at Disney he says was "phenomenal . . . like a dream come true." Or Karlos Sigueiros, head of the resort's bakery, who says he "always wanted to work at Disney," and got his chance during a two-week stint after college, which turned into a summer and became a thirty-three-year career. He brings his two girls to Disneyland every year, and his eldest wants to take over his role when he retires. There was Lisa Borotkanics, the manager of holiday services, who's in charge of the team that decorates Disney's cruise ships and has also worked for the company for thirty-three years. And Dave Caranci, who wrote a letter to Disney when he was a kid asking how he could become an "imagineer"—then eventually became one and has worked for the company for thirty-five years.

There's perhaps no better example than Disney of how successful you can be when you implement this simple strategy: hire your fans. They're the ones who know your brand, who love what you do, and who will bring a special energy to their role that an outsider may not be able to capture. Whether it's as a volunteer for a one-time event, or a long-term paid role in the leadership of the company, hiring your fans just makes a ton of sense.

For example, I've made some of the most active and helpful members of my Facebook group community administrators. One of those people is Brendan Hufford, who's been the SPI Facebook community manager for a couple of years. He helps moderate the Facebook group and gives me a pulse on what's happening in the larger community. He helps the community stay more connected.

Brendan started as a volunteer, motivated to help out by his love for the SPI community and his desire to strengthen the bonds within the community. I introduced him to everybody in the group as the admin, so he would be seen as a leader in the community. Over time, his position has evolved, and I've given him more permission to make decisions and share things with the community without asking me first—I've empowered him to do what's right for the community. With that evolution, Brendan's position has also changed from a volunteer one to a formal paid position.

Another example is John Meese, one of Michael Hyatt's team members. Michael is an incredible leadership mentor who's been a great inspiration to me on my own entrepreneurial journey. John started out as an engaged commenter on Michael's blog, but over the years he became a power user who created tutorials for Michael's "Get Noticed" WordPress theme. Eventually, Michael hired him as part of the team, and John is now the Dean of Michael's Platform University, a members-only community that helps people build their own online platforms.

There's also Staci Ardison, one of the lead trainers at Nerd Fitness, a community and coaching program that helps people break down the barriers preventing them from getting strong and healthy. Staci joined the community in 2010, looking for guidance on her own journey toward better health. She quickly felt at home, and became one of Nerd Fitness's first success stories in 2011. She then joined the Nerd Fitness coaching team, eventually becoming the lead women's coach.

Staci's path beautifully encapsulates the superfan journey, starting as a casual member of the Nerd Fitness target audience, becoming an active and increasingly engaged member of the community whose experiences and accomplishments are shared with the wider group, and flowering into a superfan who steps up to take on a leadership role on the team and eventually becomes a valuable contributor at the core of the business.

Maybe you're feeling inspired by these examples, and you want to know how to get started making your first hire or finding your first volunteer from your connected community. I'll start by telling you what *not* to do. You don't want to put a general call out saying, "Hey, who would like to be my community leader?" You're going to get a bunch of responses from people who are interested in the job for a number of different reasons. Instead, you want the process to be more organic and contained. Over time, you'll naturally start to see people lift themselves up in the community—the ones who contribute a lot and are really excited to be a part of the group—and those people, the ones who self-select for a bigger role, are the ones you should reach out to.

Once you've narrowed the candidates and started interviewing them, focus on what they can do to help you better serve the community. In this context, using words like "we" works well because it makes the person feel like they have an opportunity to be part of the team, and keeps the focus on the community you both want to serve. Ask them what they think of your ideas and what you've been doing so far, and see if they have any ideas of their own. Keep the conversation focused on the community, and on the opportunity you're offering them to help shape that community.

One important thing to keep in mind if you bring someone on as a volunteer is to make sure the relationship is fair and balanced. You don't want to ask too much of them without giving back in return, so be mindful of their workload and what you're demanding of them. At some point, though, you'll hopefully find that this person is working out so well that you'll want to look for more formal ways to compensate them. That could mean giving them more recognition among your audience, doing pro bono work for them, or offering free access to your products. And of course, there's the option of formally hiring or contracting with them.

If you don't think you're ready to bring your fans on as regular volunteers or employees, a great opportunity to get your connected community more directly involved is enlisting them to volunteer for events. Giving people in your audience the ability to influence the flow and the experience of your event can be an incredible way to bring out their inner superfan. Events I've attended, like the podcasting conferences Podfest and Podcast Movement, use volunteers to help run the show. The benefits of doing this are twofold. Of course, you can save money. But more importantly, you get to bring on people who really support the brand because they know it and they care about it. They care about the people who are there because they can relate to them. So they're going to be excited just to be a part of it. And you'll probably find that, if you put the call out, you'll have plenty of willing volunteers ready to step up.

But more than giving them a chance to feel like they're part of something exciting, it's still nice if you can compensate your dedicated event volunteers in some way, even if you're not paying them in cold, hard cash. Thankfully, there are lots of ways to repay your volunteers. You can give them free or discounted tickets to the event, and access to VIP perks. You can also thank them publicly at the event, and even bring them up on stage to introduce them to the audience.

When you make an intentional decision to cultivate your connected community into a legion of superfans, giving people the honor and responsibility of serving as a member of your team and a steward of your community will seem like a natural step. It's really a wonderful thing when your fans become integral members of your team.

This next and final story shows just what your fans can create, and the raving community of their own they can foster, when you use your influence, authority, and resources to lift them up and give them access to opportunities they wouldn't otherwise have.

The Walker Stalkers is a podcast about the TV show *The Walking Dead*. If you've never seen *The Walking Dead*, it's about a post-apocalyptic world where zombies (known as "walkers") have taken over. It centers around a number of characters who deal with crazy situations in this world—not just with the walkers, but with the other "normal" people in this world who haven't yet turned. It can get pretty insane, and I'll spare you the details in case that's not your thing. *The Walker Stalkers Podcast* was created by Eric Nordhoff and James Frazier, two guys who loved the show and wanted to celebrate their affinity for it. But the real magic started when the people behind *The Walking Dead* were willing to empower these two superfans of the show, a moment that led *The Walker Stalkers* to evolve into an incredible brand in its own right, one that has become so much more than a podcast.

The first guest Eric and James had on the podcast was Greg Nicotero, who at the time was head of makeup and effects for *The Walking Dead*. That first interview with Greg went great, and the three of them developed an easy rapport. Eric and James's connection with Greg gave them access to something other *The Walking Dead* podcasts at the time (and there were quite a few!) didn't have: the actors and crew members on the show. With Greg's help, the guys managed to book more than twenty podcast episodes in a row with actors or crew members. They also created what James calls a "light, fan-interactive atmosphere" where other fans would call in to the show to be a part of the conversation.

"We wanted the fans to be part of it," says James—also something no other *The Walking Dead* podcast was doing.

And while Eric and James were opening their podcast to fans of the show, Greg, who went on to become the show's executive producer, saw the potential value in giving these two fans access to *The Walking Dead* brand, by connecting them with others in the show's inner circle.

"He just honored us so much by giving us a good name amongst his peers," says James. In particular, through their connection with Greg, Eric and James were able to strike up a great relationship with Melissa McBride, one of the actors on the show.

With Greg and Melissa in their corner, Eric and James were set up for success in the next leg of Walker Stalker saga: creating the first Walker Stalker Con fan conference.

Walker Stalker Con started in 2013 in Atlanta, supported by a Kickstarter campaign that nearly missed its target. But it did eventually get funded, and the conference went off successfully. Over the years, thanks to the insider help of Greg and Melissa in convincing a number of other actors on the show to take part, Walker Stalker Con has grown tremendously, drawing bigger and bigger crowds of *The Walking Dead* fans and even expanding to multiple cities.

Today, Walker Stalker Con is by any measure a massive worldwide success. The 2019 schedule includes conferences in eleven different cities across the US, Europe, and Australia.

In the span of a few years, a small fan podcast turned into a hugely successful annual series of international events, all because a couple of influential people behind *The Walking Dead* brand were willing to empower those fans with the access they needed to create something magical. As a result, Eric and James, two members of *The Walking Dead*'s active audience, have created a hugely connected community of their own through their conferences and podcast. With the Walker Stalkers, *The Walking Dead* now has a legitimate worldwide brand on its side, one that's helping grow the size and enthusiasm of the show's own superfans and further cementing the show's legacy—all because one producer was shrewd enough to connect a couple of fans with some of the talented minds and icons from the show.

You can hear the full story of how Eric and James started their podcast and created the Walker Stalker Con in my conversation with them in *SPI Podcast* episode 247. Fun fact: they launched the podcast after going through some of my how-to-podcast resources! As a thank-you for helping them get their start, they gave April and me VIP tickets to the 2015 Walker Stalker Con in San Francisco. Stay tuned, because I'll tell you much more about that in the next chapter, where you'll learn how to grant your most devoted fans special access to you and your brand while simultaneously giving the rest of your audience something to aspire to: a real VIP experience.

EXERCISE

Find opportunities to get your fans involved in your brand.

STEP 1

Don't worry—this doesn't have to include making a hire if you're not ready for that move. But think about all the places where you interact with your audience and see if there are opportunities to get your most active users more involved. Do you have a Facebook group, and could you get your fans to volunteer as community moderators? Or on Instagram, could your fans volunteer to help curate some user-generated content for your feed? Has your brand been more successful in the real-life space versus the online space with meetups, and could you recruit fans to become a chapter host for your brand in their local city?

STEP 2

However you decide to make this opportunity available, decide on how you want to recruit. Will there be an application and can anyone apply? Or will it be invitation only, and you hand pick people based on how you see them engage online?

STEP 3

Start recruiting and delegating to your active users! You can establish guidelines and systems, but once your fans-turned-volunteers have things going, let them run with it and see where they take it. Always encourage them to come back to you with ideas for how things could be done better, or feedback that they hear from the wider community. You're slowly creating an army of superfans who can be your eyes and ears, extending your reach beyond where you can go on your own.

OFFER PLATINUM ACCESS

B aseball. Summertime. Sunshine. Hot dogs. The wave. Sitting in the grandstands with thousands of other raving fans who've flocked together to cheer on their favorite team. You're cramped but still pretty comfortable, and enjoying the whole scene. It's one of those quintessential experiences that never gets old.

Then you get a text from your buddy.

"Hey, are you at the game?"

"Yeah! You?"

"You bet. Where are you sitting?"

"Section 103, out in left field. You?"

"Oh, we managed to get box suite tickets. It's great! They're wining and dining us! A couple of Hall of Famers just stopped by randomly. They autographed some game balls for the kids!"

Suddenly, your quintessential summer experience starts to feel a little lackluster. It's still great, but . . . not as great as *that*.

The VIP experience—special access to unique and rare experiences and perks, like the box suite with the Hall of Famer cameos—is a superfan catalyst. It's a special tier you add to your offerings to satisfy, delight, and reward your superfans—the people who, as Kevin Kelly says, "will buy anything you produce"—and for others in your audience to aspire to.

Let's look at another example. In the past decade, Spotify has become one of the most popular music streaming services in the world—and one of the most innovative brands in terms of providing customers access to special experiences they can't get anywhere else. Through its "Fans First" program, Spotify identifies and rewards fans of various bands with early sale concert tickets, special ticket offers, exclusive merchandise, and invites to unique events.

Spotify's Fans First team works with artists to craft unique experiences and merchandise for the band's superfans, then crunches user data to figure out who those fans are. It emails the superfans with an opportunity to get in on the promotion. These promotions have included things like an intimate concert with the band Arcade Fire in New York City, or even off-the-wall events like baking cookies with singer-songwriter Ed Sheeran or afternoon tea with country artist Kacey Musgraves. They also include limited edition releases of bands' music—like the Foo Fighters, who we heard about in chapter 13, who collaborated with Spotify in 2017 to deliver a select group of fans an exclusive black-on-black vinyl pressing of their latest album, *Concrete and Gold*.

A quick search of some of the one-of-a-kind experiences Spotify has helped artists create for their biggest fans reveals how it has not only given those fans rare opportunities to get closer to their idols, but also added small touches to remind fans who's behind it all. Whether it's the all-access passes labeled "#SpotifyFansFirst" around the necks of roughly two hundred super-lucky fans of the band Interpol at the special press release in Mexico City announcing their 2018 album, or the backlit Spotify logo that graces the stage at the super-intimate Fans First concerts, these reminders help connect each magical experience in fans' minds to the brand that made it happen for them.

By allowing fans to make a rare, intimate connection with their favorite artists—and reminding them who brought it all together—Spotify is inserting itself into the connected communities of those artists' superfans, and setting those fans on their way to becoming superfans of Spotify itself.

If you go out of your way to provide your most dedicated fans with special access to events and experiences they'll never forget, you're going to cement their loyalty, whether you're a famous rock band, a music streaming service, or the creators of a series of fan conferences based on a TV show about zombies.

We ended the last chapter talking about Eric and James, the creators of *The Walker Stalkers Podcast* and the Walker Stalker Cons, all based on *The Walking Dead* TV show. Although I've liked the show ever since it debuted on Halloween 2010, I didn't really *love* it until I had my own VIP moment, one made possible because of the special access April and I were given to a Walker Stalker Con in 2015.

I'll tell you all about that in a minute—but first let me set the stage. Walker Stalker Con is a convention for *The Walking Dead* fans—sort of like Comic-Con, but for zombies. (And yes, many people dress up in zombie cosplay.) With *The Walker Stalkers Podcast* growing in popularity, Eric and James wanted to see if they could bring their fans together and put on an event. Now they host multiple conventions all over the world each year, the biggest one being in Atlanta (where the show is filmed), which attracts over twenty thousand fans. The actors of the show attend, and it's grown into quite an empire. *Inc.* magazine recently featured a story on the duo and how they turned their zombie fandom into an $11 million business. It's gotten so massive that they've even expanded it to include a Walker Stalker cruise each year.

I'm super thankful that Eric always gives me credit for inspiring him to start *The Walker Stalkers Podcast* back in 2012, which is where and how this all began.

In 2015, Eric and James gifted April and me two VIP tickets to the Walker Stalker Con taking place in San Francisco—and of course, we couldn't pass him up on this amazing offer. We didn't know what to expect, but it turned out to be one of the most memorable experiences my wife and I have ever had together.

Here's how it all unfolded.

After arriving, we were greeted by a person wearing an event shirt. To our surprise, he already knew us by name. He escorted us around the huge registration line and gave us badges with big, bold letters on the bottom that read "PLATINUM." We were already feeling pretty special at this point. Then, he showed us where the Q&A was happening—a large room with thousands of chairs, and we were going to sit right up front. He also showed us the floor where the actors and actresses were going to sign autographs, with a very clear section in each booth that said "platinum." Our passes meant we'd always get to go first, no matter how long the line was. We were also gifted a photo op with three celebrities happening later that afternoon. Finally, our escort showed us the lunch area for platinum pass holders, the same place the celebrities would be eating.

Along the way, we were introduced to a group of people dressed up as characters from the show. They were also platinum pass holders, and we later found out they were a traveling group known as Reel Guise (find them on Facebook) that goes to most of the Walker Stalker Cons together. They were all made up to look just like the characters from the show. They even had the voices down. It was amazing.

Even without platinum access, I'm sure we would have had a great time, but I'm not going to lie—it felt really awesome to have all of those extras. We had a chance to experience some things only a few others did, and it made us enjoy the conference even more. We had conversations with celebrities, we took photos, and we were treated like royalty. It made us fall totally in love with the show and cast, and, of course, with Eric and James.

That definitely wasn't the last Walker Stalker Con we've attended. Nor was it an experience we kept to ourselves. When you give your people special, platinum access, to anything, be it backstage at a concert or insider info that isn't public knowledge yet, it gives those people a huge reason to share. In addition to forging a stronger connection to the brand, the special treatment and access April and I got at the Walker Stalker Con made us feel compelled and excited to share our experience far and wide on social media.

Pat Flynn ✔
@PatFlynn

Following ⌄

At Walker Stalker Con! #WSCSF Thanks for the photo ops @Starzonboard

9:42 AM - 31 Jan 2015

5 Retweets   14 Likes

◯ 2   ⇄ 5   ♡ 14   ✉   ✦

You see, sharing happens for two main reasons:

1. Because we love to tell stories. We want to show people things they may not have seen before, to share in the excitement we experienced.
2. Because it elevates our status.

For that second reason, we can learn from a simple, yet surprising, experiment conducted by the people at the Science Channel and captured in a 2015 YouTube video.[11] A team from the Science Channel set

---

[11] Science Channel, "Would You Pay for the VIP Bus Experience?," (May 6, 2015), https://www.youtube.com/watch?v=XS6-V33kRFQ

up a velvet rope around the bench at a public bus stop, then offered people access to the "VIP bus stop experience" for $2 a pop.

It wasn't long before three men approached and were offered a chance to join the VIP section. After thinking for a few seconds, they accepted the offer and handed over $6 to cram together on the roped-off bench.

"Do you guys feel like VIPs?" asked the bouncer who had given them access.

"Yeah, it's special," said one.

"Yeah," said another one.

"It's really . . . " continued the first man, in slight awe of the experience. "You know, like, I never . . . This is a great idea."

Eventually, it dawned on the three men that the guy who'd charged them $2 each to sit sandwiched on a public bench didn't work for the transit authority, and that they'd handed over their money not because they were receiving any tangible perks in return, but simply so they could feel like they were special. They did it simply because of the self-esteem boost they'd get from feeling "roped off" from everybody else for a little while.

According to Riaz Patel, a clinical psychologist interviewed for the video, "People crave status almost as much as they crave money. The more we have status, the more we have approval. Status is a way of achieving approval without actually having to ask for it."

Thankfully, the three guys on the bench got a kick out of the whole experiment, erupting in laughter when they realized what they'd fallen for.

Now, I'm not suggesting you trick people into paying you more so they can experience the equivalent of a regular bus stop with a velvet rope around it. That would be deceptive and wrong. But you can still use this trick of human psychology to your advantage, by tapping into people's innate desire to feel special and to have an experience that's not available to everyone else.

When you're creating events, make sure to build in a VIP package that adds real, tangible value to people's overall experience. The people most likely to take you up on such an offer, and yes, pay more money for that premium experience, are your dedicated fans, the superfans and almost-superfans who see the value in the offer. But here's the thing: You're not creating those experiences only for the people who will be paying for them. You're also creating them for everyone else, by giving them a chance to see what they *could* be experiencing.

This strategy works ideally when applied to live events, like the ones we've talked about in this chapter so far, as well as in chapter 10. Bigger live events take a lot of effort and planning. And if you're going to the trouble to create your own live event, it's well worth a little extra time and effort to build in some special access opportunities for your VIPs. What could these opportunities look like for your event? Here are some ideas:

- ▶ An intimate lunch or dinner with you and a small group of others
- ▶ Early access to Q&A events
- ▶ Photo opportunities with you and other high-profile attendees
- ▶ Cool swag like signed books

In fact, several of those items are things I made available to VIP attendees at the first FlynnCon in 2019. I got this model by learning from VIP experiences other entrepreneurs have created for their own events, like the ones Chalene Johnson has offered at her Marketing Impact Academy and Smart Success Summit events. At these conferences, Chalene's VIPs get access to the rooms early, front row seating at tables, time for pictures with Chalene, a special party just for them, and an exclusive Q&A with Chalene.

In fact, when I was putting together FlynnCon, a number of people told me it would have been nuts *not* to offer this kind of special access, because it's precisely the kind of experience that superfans and almost-superfans want and expect from such an event—even if it may seem ridiculous to others.

Thankfully, the barriers to entry to creating your own platinum access experience are much lower than you might expect. You can easily have swag made, like t-shirts, bags, pins, and even action figurines. Setting up things like early access to Q&As, photo ops, and even VIP meals mostly requires a little advanced planning, but not that much in the way of logistics. Trust me: The lion's share of your time and energy is going to be spent putting on the event as a whole, so once you've got the foundation down, adding these perks on top is not going to be a huge deal for you—but it will definitely be one for the fans who take you up on that VIP experience.

Need a little more inspiration for how to create a VIP package for your next event? Check out the two options for a VIP experience at LEGOLAND California Resort:[12]

ULTIMATE VIP EXPERIENCE

BUDDY VIP EXPERIENCE

- Admission to LEGOLAND® California and SEA LIFE® Aquarium
- Personal VIP host to escort you around the Park for the entire day
- Exclusive Behind-the-Scenes experiences (see options under Behind-the-Scenes)
- Priority access to all rides, shows and attractions
- Interesting and unknown Park and LEGO® Model facts
- Minifigure for trading
- Valet parking at the LEGOLAND Hotel
- Lunch and refreshments (alcohol not included)
- Souvenir photo package
- LEGOLAND gift

- Admission to LEGOLAND® California
- Personal VIP host to escort you around the Park during your experience
- Priority access to rides and attractions
- Interesting and unknown Park and LEGO® Model Facts
- Minifigure for trading
- Lunch at Pizza & Pasta Buffet

Priority access, cool gear, a meal or two . . . totally doable, right?

Or take a cue from what's on offer in one of the coolest premium packages I've seen, the "Jedi Master VIP" option for the 2019 Star Wars Celebration in Chicago, an annual fan gathering billed as "the ultimate Star Wars fan festival." This festival has taken place each year since 1999 in a different city, and it's a weekend-long Star Wars experience featuring cast and crew appearances, Star Wars cosplay, exclusive merchandise, live

---

[12] "VIP EXPERIENCES," (Accessed April 22, 2019), https://www.legoland.com/california/legoland-california/buy-tickets/vip-experiences.

entertainment, screenings, behind-the-scenes panels, exhibits, and "never-before-seen glimpses into the future of Star Wars."[13]

∧ Details

The Jedi Master VIP Package Includes:

- One (1) Jedi Master VIP Badge Featuring Exclusive Art
- One (1) Official Show Poster (Rolled, complete with poster tube)
- One (1) Commemorative Program Guide
- VIP Lounge with coat check and concierge
- Half Hour Early Access to Exhibit Hall
- Half Hour Early Access to the Official Celebration Store each day
- Exclusive Celebration Store private shopping experience on Thursday, April 11 at 11:00 AM
- VIP Express Checkout Lane at the Official Celebration Store
- Unlimited use of the Lightspeed Lane to enter the Official Celebration Store
- Express Autograph Hall Autograph line pass and checkout for up to six (6) Autograph Sessions. Price of Autographs not included.
- First Access to Panels at the Celebration Stage
  - We will be clearing the Celebration Stage after each panel, Jedi Masters will have first access to seats for each panel on the Celebration Stage. There will be no reserved seating, but you will have first choice of seats for each Panel on the Celebration Stage. You MUST arrive at least 40 minutes prior to the start of any Celebration Stage Panel you wish to attend.
- One (1) Private Meet & Greet with select Star Wars Celebration guest or guests
  - Guest determined at the discretion of *Star Wars* Celebration and to be announced at a later date.
- One (1) Original signed art print, created exclusively for Celebration Chicago Jedi Master VIPs
- One (1) Extremely Limited Jedi Master VIP character pin shared only, in very limited amounts, with staff as a giveaway pin that will not otherwise be made available for sale to *Star Wars* Celebration Chicago Attendees.
- One (1) Exclusive Jedi Master VIP Lanyard
- One (1) Exclusive Jedi Master VIP Embroidered Patch
- One time 10% off discount at the Official Celebration Store

The screenshot of all the perks kind of speaks for itself—that's an awesome list of items and experiences. But again, they almost all fall into a couple of the categories we've already outlined: early and exclusive access to events, along with cool swag. This is a pretty impressive-looking list that would make any Star Wars superfan swoon, but trust me: You can pull off something like this, too.

That brings me to my final point, which is that creating a platinum access experience should never—I repeat, never—come at the expense of the experience for the general attendee. The baseline experience you provide for people should always be awesome—you just want to offer something that's even more awesome for the people, the devoted fans in your

13 "Ticket Details," (Accessed April 22, 2019), https://www.starwarscelebration.com/About/Ticket-Details.

audience, who are willing to pay for it. A truly honorable VIP experience is one in which you make sure that you're not compromising the integrity of the connected community by creating a huge gulf between your VIPs and the rest of the attendees; you're just giving those VIPs special perks and access here and there.

The VIPs get to enjoy the same delicious cupcake everyone else is eating. Theirs just has a cherry on top.

One of the best parts of this strategy is that you don't have to host a big event to put it into action—even a birthday party can suffice. Kevin Schneider is a resident of Evanston, Illinois, in his forties with a developmental disability. He's also a superfan of the sport teams at Northwestern University in Chicago. As of 2012, he managed to attend roughly fifty or sixty Northwestern athletic events each year.

He was also a fixture in the athletic department's offices, someone whose joy and love for sports radiated from him. According to Northwestern's then associate director of athletic communications, Doug Meffley, Kevin was an ever-present part of the scene. "Somewhere along the line, [Kevin] just became part of the fabric around here. I don't know a Northwestern that Kevin wasn't a part of."

All the way back in 1990, Kevin started collecting schedule cards for all the teams Northwestern played. When one of Northwestern's squads went on the road, Kevin asked them to bring him back cards from all the teams in the area. But it wasn't always easy or possible to get cards for Kevin, given time and travel constraints.

The folks at Northwestern wanted to do something to thank and reward Kevin for his immense support—and helping him fill out his schedule card collection seemed like the perfect opportunity. So, for Kevin's birthday in 2012, one of the staff members in the athletic department decided to launch a Schedule Cards for Kevin campaign. To support the campaign, Meffley wrote a blog post asking Northwestern alumni and fans to pick up schedule cards at their local games and drop them in the mail for Kevin.

Meffley didn't expect much of a response—but he was blown away by what happened.

"Little by little, packages and cards started coming in, and as it continued to be shared and show up on different blogs, the trickle became a flood," Meffley says. In all, the campaign brought in approximately five hundred envelopes and packages, containing many thousands of schedule cards.

Meffley and the athletic department threw Kevin a thirty-sixth birthday party where they presented him with the cards. It was the perfect way to thank this ultimate fan for the love and joy he'd brought to Northwestern athletics for decades.[14]

By now, you've likely already developed some superfans, so give them the VIP experience they crave—and give the other dedicated fans in your audience a superfan nudge, something to look up to and plan for the next time they attend your event.

---

[14] You can read more about Kevin's story at http://www.thepostgame.com/blog/good-sports/201209/kevin-schneider-northwestern-wildcats-schedule-cards.

EXERCISE

Create your own VIP experience.

STEP 1

Brainstorm your VIP offering. Consider what you could do to thank and delight the small number of highly engaged members of your audience. It doesn't have to be huge or extravagant to start. And don't worry if you aren't at the event-hosting stage (or don't want to be). VIP experiences don't have to be exclusive to in-person events. Do you sell digital products or online courses? If so, could you create a VIP version of those products that includes additional value, like access to you in some way—perhaps via a private webinar or livestream Q&A. What's something you *wish* you could offer your entire community, but would be hard to give everyone? You could make this VIP experience something people have to pay for, or a bonus for something they're already getting.

STEP 2

Get feedback. Ask for input from mentors or your mastermind or other people you trust. Ask for input from your audience. It can be as simple and casual as, "Hey I'm thinking about making this extra offering available as a VIP version of my flagship product. What are your thoughts?"

STEP 3

Finalize the details, make the offering available, and announce it to your audience! You may want to consider only sharing this opportunity with a select few in your audience, and even go as far as to make it invite-only first.

LET'S GO DEEPER

As a reminder, there are a lot of links in this chapter, and in this book. To get easy access to all of the links and resources mentioned for each chapter, make sure you visit **yoursuperfans.com/course**.

W e've made it! We've traced the entire superfan journey, from casual visitors having their earliest interactions with your brand, to active subscribers and followers interested in hearing from you regularly, to engaged and connected members of your community willing to bring you, your brand, and your people closer to their heart, to dedicated superfans who live and breathe your brand and find a true home in your community. And all along the way, we've uncovered numerous strategies to cultivate and energize those *inner* superfans until they become *outer* superfans.

Keep in mind that these strategies are a soft science, not a hard science. People won't necessarily proceed orderly through these four stages—they're not taking a test! And not every fan who comes across you will become a superfan, no matter what you do, while some of them will leapfrog the early stages we covered in this book and go right to raving superfan the first time they make a real connection with you and what you have to offer them.

There's one more area we need to cover, and it's not exactly the fun part of building superfans. But it's crucial, and so address it we must. In the next part, we'll go over the dark side of building superfans: why the stakes are higher when you have superfans, and what can go wrong as you're building a devoted audience. But of course, and most importantly, we'll also go over what you need to know and do to avoid these pitfalls that can befall you as you develop a circle of fans who love you and everything you do.

PART 4

THE DARK SIDE OF BUILDING SUPERFANS

SUPERFANS

CONNECTED

ACTIVE

CASUAL

W e've come a long way in our journey together, and you've learned a lot. You've discovered how you can grab the attention of casual audience members finding you for the first time and start cultivating them into active members of your tribe who will keep coming back for more. You've unlocked the ability to nurture these people into a connected community and build experiences that will get them more involved and invested. Finally, you've uncovered how to create those extra-special moments that turn connected community members into raving super-fans who will stick by your side through thick and thin.

In the words of Uncle Ben Parker from the *Spider-Man* series, "With great power comes great responsibility." With these superfans comes great power—power that must be balanced.

As you build your brand and create those special moments that will mold people into superfans, you're also going to encounter some danger-ous traps that threaten to strip away some or all of the fruits of the hard work you're putting in. That's why we need to spend some time talking about the biggest pitfalls you need to look out for if you want to keep your fans at the top of the pyramid, cheering you on forever.

Whether or not you already have a devoted group of überfans, these final two chapters are crucial reading. Here's what we'll cover:

- ► **CHAPTER 18: THE 6 HIDDEN TRAPS OF BUILDING SUPERFANS–AND HOW TO AVOID THEM**
- ► **CHAPTER 19: AVOIDING UNWANTED RECOGNITION AND STAYING SAFE**

THE 6 HIDDEN TRAPS OF BUILDING SUPERFANS— AND HOW TO AVOID THEM

When you attempt to do something worthwhile, like building and serving an audience of dedicated superfans, there will be downsides and dark sides. In this chapter, I'll highlight the six biggest traps you might find yourself in when building an audience of superfans, and how to avoid them.

Trap 1: You get a chip on your shoulder.

When you have a big audience paying close attention to everything you say and do, you have to be thoughtful about the messages you put out there—and be willing to let some things slide. Back when my daughter Kai was almost two, she was starting to outgrow her crib and getting really excited about having a real "big kid" bed. So we promised her a bed for her birthday. We ordered one from Pottery Barn, but when it arrived, there was just a headboard in the box. Kai was pretty upset, and so was I. So I decided to take to Twitter to give Pottery Barn an earful (tweetful?) about how they'd ruined my daughter's birthday.

But as soon as I hit return on the tweet, a number of people replied back saying, "Pat, this sort of thing happens to all of us. Can you get off your high horse here?"

The almost immediate negative responses were like a splash of cold water to the face. They reminded me that everyone goes through stuff like this from time to time, and although people were sorry to hear Kai had been upset about the bed, they also made it clear that I was being negative and whiny. After twelve or fifteen replies in that vein, I decided, rather than delete the tweet, that I'd keep it public. Instead, I apologized and owned up to the fact that I was being petty and entitled by choosing to complain. Thankfully, several people replied back acknowledging that I'd owned up to my mistake and showed that I learned from it.

Bottom line: You can still make mistakes and keep your fans. The key is to be aware when you've done something wrong. If you misstep and people react negatively, the first thing to do is slow down and pay attention; don't just react. Assess the situation calmly. Listen to what people are saying, then take your time to respond in a thoughtful way. People will see that you've taken their comments to heart, and most will probably appreciate you for it.

Above all, hold yourself to a high standard. Not in the sense that you should act like you're better than anyone else, because you're not. But because your words and actions are naturally going to be noticed, so you have to put a lot of care into what you put out there. When you have a big following, you have to remember how every word and every action represents the brand you've built. It may require some soul searching and discomfort to come back from a mishap, but it's still possible to save face and earn back trust if you're honest and act according to your core values.

Trap 2: You let the fame and money get to your head.

SPI's chief operating officer (COO), Matt Gartland, has his own powerful superfan story—this one from the world of sports—about what can happen when you let the fame and acclaim that emerges when you build an audience of super-dedicated fans go to your head.

Matt grew up in Pittsburgh and remains a loyal fan of the "black-and-gold"—the Pittsburgh Steelers. The Steelers are near and dear to almost everyone from the Steel City, and wide receiver Antonio Brown was "a special person on a special team," Matt says. Over the years, "AB" racked up the stats and accolades, earning him superstar status in the NFL. He became a fan favorite, and Matt's favorite too. Matt even has an autographed football from AB in his office, something Matt considers "a symbol of greatness—the work ethic it takes to become the best at one's craft, especially when others doubt you (as most did when AB entered the league)."

AB was a shining light for Pittsburgh, with a city's worth of superfans rallying around him.

But problems began when AB's fame started to get in the way of his relationship with the Steelers, and even between him and his fans. There was the occasional provocative celebration in the endzone following a touchdown. Then tensions grew when Antonio was reported to be habitually late to mandatory team meetings. They got worse when off-the-field issues began to surface involving borderline violent behaviors. And eventually, they escalated into a power struggle between AB and his quarterback, as well as him and his coach.

Ultimately, the tensions exploded at the end of the 2018–19 season, leaving Antonio benched for the final regular season game and causing a firestorm in the media that culminated bitterly in a trade to the Oakland Raiders. A year before that, Antonio was on a trajectory to become the next Jerry Rice, one of the greatest wide receivers to have ever played. But since AB's relationship with his team and his fans started going downhill, Matt says people no longer talk about AB in such glowing terms. He says the conversation has shifted to comparisons with players like Terrell Owens and Chad (Ocho Cinco) Johnson, "talented wide receivers in their own right but players generally regarded by professional sports reporters and fans alike as more self-interested divas than stalwart champions who are among the greatest of all time."

(If you haven't been able to figure it out, Matt is a *huge* football fan.)

The higher they fly, the harder they can fall. Matt says the whole situation is such a shame, one that he and many other former superfans of AB feel deeply.

At the same time, he realizes that not everyone in Pittsburgh has handed in their AB superfan card. Plenty of Steel Citizens feel betrayed by their former hero, but some fans have also stuck by AB's side. "Just like his relationship with the Steelers, his relationship with his fanbase has fractured. Some are vehemently taking his side in the saga. Others, like me, are not."

Still, says Matt, "Lots and lots and lots of fans have turned against AB. If you know of someone who hasn't, let me know because I have a football I'd like to sell them."

Few of us will ever find ourselves in the same position as Antonio Brown. But as you become more known in your own world or niche, some of that celebrity energy can start to take over, and it can get to your head.

I'll tell you a story of my own. Once upon a time, I had two friends in the online business world. They started their own business together around the same time I fired up Smart Passive Income, and we helped each other navigate this challenging new world. We chatted online a lot and even met in person a few times. We were all trying to figure out this online business thing, and it was great to have each other to lean on and share business advice. I considered them my friends.

After some time, their businesses started to take off. They were making money and developing a name in the entrepreneurial space. I was excited for their success. But I wasn't excited about how the success was changing who they were. The attention and the money started to get to their heads. Their behavior changed. They became self-centered, like everything was owed to them. It became clear that the money and fame were more important to them than relationships.

They also started automating a lot of the transactions and interactions with their audience, which I think contributed to this negative shift. Of course, there's nothing wrong with automation, per se. It's important to systematize things as you get bigger, or you're not going to keep up or be able to serve your audience as well as you could. But when you forget about the relationship aspect and focus too much on the money and prestige—then add over-automation into the mix, where you're cut off from your audience—that's a recipe for disaster.

Today, I no longer consider them my friends. I haven't spoken to them in nearly eight years. I'm not sure how their businesses are doing, but they're no longer a household name in the space they were in before.

Always remember why you're building an audience: to serve people. If you can make lots of money and become famous doing that, great. If you need to automate some things to better serve your audience, great. Just remember that your success is fundamentally about the relationships you've built. When you lose sight of the meaningful interactions and special moments that bring your audience closer to you, you're going to push people away, and your business will suffer.

Trap 3: You don't plan properly—with unintended consequences.

Here's a lesson for business and for life in general: your intentions may not always match their outcomes. Your actions can sometimes have unforeseen consequences or come off the wrong way. To put it another way, you may not realize you're sending the wrong message to your audience—especially when it comes to your marketing—if you're not planning appropriately and taking a big-picture view of things.

There were points early in my online business journey when I was sending lots of sales emails pretty close together. I wasn't trying to oversell my products—I just wasn't giving enough thought to how I should be spacing out my promotions. At the time, it was out of sight, out of mind for me. But the effect of those emails on my audience, regardless of my intention, was negative—and they let me know it. A lot of people emailed me back making it clear that this wasn't cool. Some of them even told me they felt like I was slipping into the dark side of internet marketing, focusing too much on selling and not enough on helping people succeed without expecting anything in return.

It was a wake-up call, for sure.

I realized that I wasn't planning things the right way. I wasn't spacing my promotions appropriately, and even though I wasn't *trying* to sell to people all the time, that's how it came across. But with the help of my team, we implemented a content calendar that allowed us to see all the different content types we were publishing over the course of a year, and better determine if the promotional content was spaced out properly. It's often the mundane process-related things, like a twelve-month content calendar, that help you see what you're actually doing and whether it's serving your audience—and can save you from the trap of unintended consequences.

But more than that, it was my biggest fans who were the most outspoken about this misstep—because they cared enough to let me know what I was doing. They didn't want to see the brand they had gotten behind take a turn for the worse. And that's what's so great about having superfans: they can help steer the ship when it gets off course, because they're so invested in the direction it's been heading.

Trap 4: Other people's actions reflect badly on you.

Even the mistakes of others can come back to haunt you and turn fans against you. The biggest buffer against this is to be selective about who you associate yourself with. But sometimes you just can't tell until it's too late, and you have to be prepared for the possibility that someone else's actions could bring you down.

Back in 2010, I was really focused on building niche websites, which are sites designed to help people looking for information on a specific topic. The idea is to create a site that will rank high in search results for a few specific keywords, then make money on the site through products and advertisements.

That year, I agreed to participate in a "niche site duel" with a fellow entrepreneur in the online business space. He challenged me to a competition in which we would each build a niche site and see if we could make it more successful than the other person's.

After some research, I picked my niche (security guard training) and went to work. It worked out pretty well! I got my new site, SecurityGuardTrainingHQ.com, to rank number one in Google after seventy-three days for the keyword "security guard training." The site continues to rank highly and make money even today.

But in the beginning, having a fun site-building contest with my friend was the main focus. We were essentially playing a game to see who could make the most money from our site. We also agreed to be transparent with each other and our audiences about the whole process—how we were building the sites, how much traffic they were getting, and how much money we were making.

Things were going fine for a while, with both of us creating our sites and sharing our progress with everyone. But a few months after we started the duel, he posted a video admitting that he'd been exaggerating some of his numbers. He'd been lying to everyone. He said he felt guilty about it and wanted to come clean.

I was shocked. I was thankful that he'd decided to be truthful about the deception, but still hurt and surprised that he'd done it in the first place—and taken me along for the ride.

As soon as the video came out, I started getting emails from people saying, "How could you be associated with this person? I don't know if I can trust you anymore." It was a really tough time for me. I had to end my relationship with him, and definitely lost some fans. For a while, it cast a shadow on my brand and how people perceived me. As for him, he basically lost his entire audience and had to drop off the radar for a while. Eventually he started up in an entirely different industry.

You can't control the actions of others, or the reactions of your audience to those actions. And despite your best judgment, people may not turn out to be who you thought they were. It's true in life, and it's true in business. This is one of those traps you'll never be able to totally avoid, but being aware of that possibility may help you.

Trap 5: You try to respond to everybody.

Over time, as your audience begins to grow, you simply won't be able to respond to every single person who reaches out to you as much as you'd like to.

I have personal experience with this. Early on, I loved being able to respond to every message I got—email, social media, you name it. But eventually, the increasing responsibility of building a business took its toll, and I stopped being able to respond to everyone. I had to give it up, or I wouldn't have had time to get anything else done. This happened to me when I was working on my Green Exam Academy site, and even more so when Smart Passive Income became my focus.

In both cases, it was really hard. I felt like I was letting people down.

If you find yourself in this boat, it's not a disaster. Don't feel bad. In fact, it's a natural part of growing an audience and building a business. Be realistic, and know that you can still address and interact with your audience in different ways, just not exactly how you used to. Here are the strategies I've used to stay in touch with my audience even though I can no longer respond to every single email, tweet, and DM.

- ▶ Conduct one-to-many conversations. These can be on social media, in webinars, on live streams, and at live events.
- ▶ Highlight and address questions from specific people and share them with everyone. Although you can't speak one-on-one with everyone, doing it with a few people and sharing it still makes you relatable and like you're interacting with your community.
- ▶ Hire team members who can help with audience communication and interaction. This will help people feel like you're still paying attention to them (because you are!). Consider bringing on people (moderators and admins) to help with email and social media in particular.

On that last point, here's one of the best tips I can give you: don't have your team members pretend to be you. Sometimes it'll be really obvious that you're doing this, and it'll always come across as insincere. The answer is to hire the right people, ones who align with your values (like your fans—see chapter 16), then train them to support and engage with your audience the way you'd like. Your team members need to be your representatives, not your stunt doubles.

Trap 6: You burn out.

Being an entrepreneur is an exciting ride. It can also be a recipe for exhaustion and burnout. As you begin to build fans and encounter new opportunities to grow your business, you can be tempted to say yes to everything, and quickly find yourself in a hole. If you've ever tried to run your own business and build a fanbase, there's a good chance that at some point you've come close to or reached the point of burnout, or known someone else who has.

It's no fun.

In 2016, *Huffington Post* founder Arianna Huffington told *Entrepreneur* about her own scary experience with burnout. In 2007, after a long period of sleep deprivation, she collapsed in her office. She found herself on the floor, her face covered in blood and her cheekbone broken from hitting the side of her desk on the way down.

"It was a question of coming to in a pool of blood and realizing nobody had shot me," she says.

Huffington went through a battery of tests to find out what was wrong with her, but was eventually given the diagnosis of burnout.

She says she "listened to the wakeup call" and started prioritizing sleep—eight hours a night, compared to four or five before. Since then, she's written a book called *The Sleep Revolution* and become a huge advocate for the importance of sleep, especially for people like startup founders, tech workers, and other ambitious people who don't realize they can't run on fumes forever.

"I'm very grateful that it happened because I think it could have been much worse," says Huffington.

She is, sadly, far from the only person who's dealt with burnout as a result of working too hard. On several occasions, I've shared the story of my friend and fellow entrepreneur Chris Ducker, who spent ten days in the hospital after burning out trying to wear all the hats in his growing business.

Although I've never faced full-blown burnout myself, I've come close. When it comes to staying away from that ledge, what can you do? Here are four things that help me a lot.

Get sleep. Sleep is when your body gets a chance to rest and your brain does some cleanup. The brain is actually highly active during parts of the sleep cycle, consolidating memories, processing emotions, and cleaning out waste products. Basically, if you don't get enough sleep, your brain won't work properly. And what good is that extra hour or two of work time if you're operating below capacity? Another great book I recommend for learning how to sleep better is my friend Shawn Stevenson's book, *Sleep Smarter*, which helped me change the quality of my sleep, literally overnight.

Don't do it all yourself. Don't ignore the little voice warning you not to bite off more than you can chew! As Arianna Huffington says in her 2016 interview with *Entrepreneur*, "Building the *Huffington Post*, I bought into the mythology that everything was dependent on me and I had to do everything at the expense of sleep, health . . . "[15] As you're building your business and your audience of superfans, you're going to hit points where you'll need to delegate and ask for help (see trap 5).

Lean on your support network. Whether it's family, friends, your team, your mastermind group, your church, or your bowling team. If you're struggling and worried you're about to burn out, don't be afraid to talk to somebody. Your support network can also be a

---

[15] Catherine Clifford, "Arianna Huffington's Dramatic Lesson After 'Coming to in a Pool of Blood and Realizing Nobody Had Shot Me'," (Jul 5, 2016), https://www.entrepreneur.com/video/278593.

great resource to let you know if you're showing signs of burnout that you may not notice yourself. They can be a shoulder to lean on when you're having trouble, and a reality check when you're working too hard to see the bigger picture.

Stay focused on what matters. Remember why you got into business and decided to build an audience in the first place. For me, it's serving my audience and supporting my family, and leading by example for both my audience and my kids. Staying focused on what's truly important will help you see things clearly when you're in the weeds working on your business. To help you keep your perspective, it can be really helpful to have a daily practice that takes you out of the headspace and intensity of work. For me it's meditation, while for others it might be a walk outside or a session in the gym.

These six traps aren't the only ones you might encounter as you build your audience and cultivate them into superfans—not even close—but they're the biggest ones I've seen and dealt with myself over the past decade. I hope that by being aware of them and how you can avoid (or at least reduce the impact of) them, you're in a better position to serve your audience and maintain the trust you're building with your fans.

There's one final idea I want to talk about before we sign off on this chapter, and that idea is *change*. Change is inevitable, and often it's messy. Over time, you're going to evolve, and so will your brand. But when you change who you are at the core, guess what'll happen? Your fans will notice. And they'll make a decision about whether the change makes them feel more or less connected to you. That's not to say you shouldn't change for the better; you're going to grow, and honestly, some of your fans simply aren't going to stay with you forever, no matter what you do. But if change means compromising your values and the things people have come to love you for, then why would even your true fans want to stay along for the ride?

The journey to the top of the pyramid is a hard one, but just because you've earned your fans doesn't mean they're going to stay there forever. As hard as it is to create a superfan, it can be much easier to lose one. Remember this twist on the timeless *Spider-Man* quote: with great fans comes great responsibility.

In the next chapter, we'll talk about why not all attention is good attention, and how to keep yourself and the people you love safe as your audience is growing.

AVOIDING UNWANTED RECOGNITION AND STAYING SAFE

As you expand your brand and build stronger, deeper relationships with your audience, you may become a celebrity in the eyes of some of your fans. Because of that, it's important to understand the safety hazards that may present themselves, and how certain important decisions you make now can affect your safety and the safety of those close to you.

Some fans will go to great lengths to get closer to their favorite celebrities. Instead of a team of hired paparazzi trying to grab a golden photo for tomorrow's tabloids, they're merely superfans who want a golden memory to keep and share. Unfortunately, some of these fans often cross the line.

In December 2018, James Charles, a nineteen-year old YouTuber with over fifteen million subscribers as of the writing of this book, was trending in headlines all over the world thanks to this tweet:

James Charles ✓
@jamescharles

(Follow) ⌄

please stop showing up at my house. i will not hug you, i will not take a photo with you, and i absolutely will not sign your palette. it is extremely disrespectful & makes me feel very unsafe in my own home. respect people's privacy, it's really not that hard.

3:13 PM - 16 Dec 2018

James let the world know he was feeling unsafe in his own home after several fans showed up at his house hoping to get a picture or catch a glimpse of the YouTube superstar.

He's not the only one. I've seen similar announcements by other popular YouTube personalities, like one of my kids' favorites, Daniel Middleton, better known as DanTDM. A young British YouTuber with over twenty-one million subscribers who creates a lot of gaming-related videos, he tweeted something similar at the beginning of 2018:

DanTDM 💎 ✓
@dantdm

(Follow) ⌄

Guys, I love you, but please don't turn up at mine or my family's house, knocking on the door and shouting for me to come out.
I won't.
My house is my personal space and isn't the right place to meet me.
Thank you for understanding :) 👊 💎

10:00 AM - 7 Jan 2018

In both cases, this behavior is obviously not okay. Most of the people in James's case seemed to be younger kids—but that makes me wonder about the parents who took them to James's house. C'mon, parents! Don't we look out for each other's kids?

I don't share these examples to scare you, but because this is a topic we must cover.

Here's the thing: *Most* fans are considerate and will respect your space and privacy. Both James and DanTDM had tens of thousands of fans step up to express anger with the few people in the audience who were disrespecting their heroes. But it only takes a very small percentage of your audience to cross the line and make life difficult, or even scary for you.

Even if you don't have millions of subscribers, you still need to take the right precautions to make sure you stay safe along the way.

I didn't realize the importance of this until one of my fans decided to dig into my Instagram account and found my home address by geolocating some of the pictures I'd shared from my home office. Luckily, he was actually looking out for my safety and brought the oversight to my attention quickly. Soon after, I removed all of the photos from my Instagram Photo Map, which easily gave away my location for all of the photos I was taking. Since then, Photo Map has been removed from Instagram's feature list, so this particular issue is not something you have to worry about anymore, but there are other ways people can find details of your life that you might prefer to keep private. That's why it's best to consider the following tips sooner than later.

1. Do not use your home address in your business, EVER.

The best practice is to always separate home and business operations as much as humanly possible. Even if you work from home, having a separate business address makes sense. You'll be asked to provide an address when signing up for a domain name, email service provider, and other important services you need to run your business.

Unless you purchase domain privacy (also known as WhoIS privacy), did you know that the address and other information you use to register your domain name is accessible to the public? A simple search at https://whois.icann.org can reveal the address and even name and phone number of the person who registered a domain. Domain privacy ($10–

$20 per year) will hide that information from the public. If you're currently using your home address on your domain (and now would be a good time to check!), don't worry. Either purchase domain privacy through your registrar, or use a business (non-home) address instead.

When it comes to your business's mailing address, all business-related mail should be sent to an address that's not your home address. Which prompts the question: where might one obtain such an address? Luckily, you have a few options:

Your local UPS Store. UPS Store mailboxes give you an address of the store and a suite number that matches your mailbox number. This was the first address I ever had outside of my own home that I still use to this day for many business-related items, especially shipping. UPS does a great job of holding packages, and it's convenient when I pick up mail every few weeks to utilize their services to send anything I need to send. The cost of a UPS mailbox depends on the size of the box you use, but I recommend sticking with the smallest size, which runs a few hundred dollars a year.

A local coworking space that has mail and package handling. I'm a member of WeWork, a worldwide coworking space with multiple locations that I love, and most have a mail and package handling option that you can add to your membership for a monthly fee. Check coworking spaces in your local area for mail and package handling options, and make sure you're able to obtain an address when you register for it.

Virtual office spaces. These are similar to coworking spaces but don't usually provide the same amenities. They often have receptionists and meeting areas that can be rented, and some also offer a professional business address.

One question people often ask when trying to get a business address: Can you use a United States Postal Service (USPS) PO Box? You can for most things, but if you're looking to register an official business address with your state in the US, they will not accept a PO Box as an official address for your business. You may use it for things like your domain name and email service provider, but even then it's better to get something that looks more official from some of the other options above.

You may also, depending on your business structure, be required to have a real physical address for something called a *registered agent*. This is a person you designate as someone who can accept important paperwork about your business, like government or legal documents. Every state in the US requires that an incorporated business appoint a registered agent for the entity, and that agent must have a physical address in that state.

You are allowed to be your own registered agent, but you will be required to supply your home address to the state, not your business address—and unfortunately, registered agents and their information are indeed public information.

The workaround is appointing a third party as your registered agent. Mine is my attorney, and this is what I recommend you do too, if you have one. If not, there are third-party companies that offer such a service; search Google for "[name of state] registered agent service," and be sure to look at a large number of results, as prices can vary widely.

2. Create rules for location sharing on social media.

We don't have to worry about Instagram's photo mapping feature anymore, which unknowingly made it easy for anyone to see where your photos were taken, but you do still have the option of sharing your location on every post you publish on Instagram and other social media platforms like Facebook, Twitter, and LinkedIn.

I share my location when it makes sense, and usually only after I've left. If I'm going somewhere for business, I may be a bit more lax—I'll share the location of a conference I'm speaking at or the airport I happen to be traveling through. However, when I'm with my family, even if we're not at home, I hardly ever share my location, and if I do, it's usually long after we've left.

We're all going to have different levels of comfort. These are the rules I've set for myself, but you should consider what you're comfortable with when it comes to your privacy and safety, especially if you have family and others to consider.

And these rules don't have to be complicated—as long as you follow them consistently. One time, a friend called me out for sharing my route via Nike's running app. I was proud of my ten-mile run, one of the milestones in my triathlon training, and after sharing a map of the run on social media, he called me to let me know I'd just given everyone the location of my home. It was a bit scary, but he was right, and I hadn't even realized what I was doing.

3. Make sure you don't photograph or film these things by accident.

Sometimes, without even knowing it, you may be revealing valuable information that could compromise your privacy. When filming or shooting photography, be sure to watch out for these following items, which a person could hypothetically use to track your location:

- ▶ Vehicle license plate
- ▶ Home numbers
- ▶ Home address on packages sent to you
- ▶ Home address on letters you receive or send
- ▶ Pictures of the outside of your home (via reverse photo search— remember, Google has likely driven by and taken a picture of your home for Google Maps)

I once filmed a drone video outside my house, and for just a split second, the license plate of our minivan was shown on screen. Two people emailed me later that day to say they might be able to find our address because of that license plate, and I believe that to be true. Of course, immediately after they told me about the situation, I removed the video from my social channels, and all was fine. Again, I'm thankful that these fans were looking out for my best interests, and that it ended up being a minor lesson I can pass on to you now.

Luckily, I've never had an encounter with disrespectful fans or anyone doing something out of line (although I have had my fair share of run-ins with weirdos at events I've attended, stories I'll save for another day), but I've been getting recognized in public for a few years now.

My first encounter was in a Trader Joe's parking lot. As I was loading groceries into my car, someone walked up to me and asked in an excited and curious voice, "Are you Pat Flynn?"

"Yes . . . " I said nervously until I was greeted with a barrage of praise for my podcast and work. I shook his hand, then sat in the car wondering what the heck had just happened. It was cool, but also scary at the same time. It was surprising, and it made me realize that I mattered to people. A ton of feelings all wrapped into one encounter—and I never even caught the person's name.

One of my favorite encounters happened at a Cold Stone Creamery while waiting for ice cream with my family and in-laws. Out of nowhere, a woman came up to me and told me she was a raving fan and loved everything I did, and even that I'd helped change her life. After she left, the look on my in-laws' face was priceless—I think it was a mixture of "Who the heck was that?" and "Who the heck did our daughter marry?"

At events, the recognition is dialed up quite a bit. Because many of my fans attend the same conferences where I speak, sometimes it's hard to even walk through the hallways without getting bombarded with attention. I love it, but I don't think I'll ever get used to it. I always do my best, however, to talk to every single person I can. I once stayed in the halls at an event for five hours straight to say hello to everyone waiting in line to chat. I do feel drained when it's all over, and to get me back into my energy zone, as an introvert, I have to lock myself in my hotel room for a few hours or the rest of the night, get under the covers, turn on Netflix, and just escape.

All this is to say: Even if you don't think it'll happen, it could, and I want you to be prepared if it does. Use common sense, and most of all, enjoy the attention! Be proud of it! You might feel awkward that people care about you so much, but they do for a reason. Most likely they love you for what you've given them, whether it be inspiration, hope, guidance, laughter, or entertainment. Celebrate what you've accomplished and who you've been able to make an impact on. That's what I remember each time someone comes up to me at an event or in public: not that I'm this amazing celebrity everyone should know about (because I'm not), but that my work allows me to help people, and that motivates me to help even more folks who may need what I have to offer.

Just remember, as you grow, stay proud but grounded, and don't let it get to your head.

YOUR SUPERFANS AWAIT

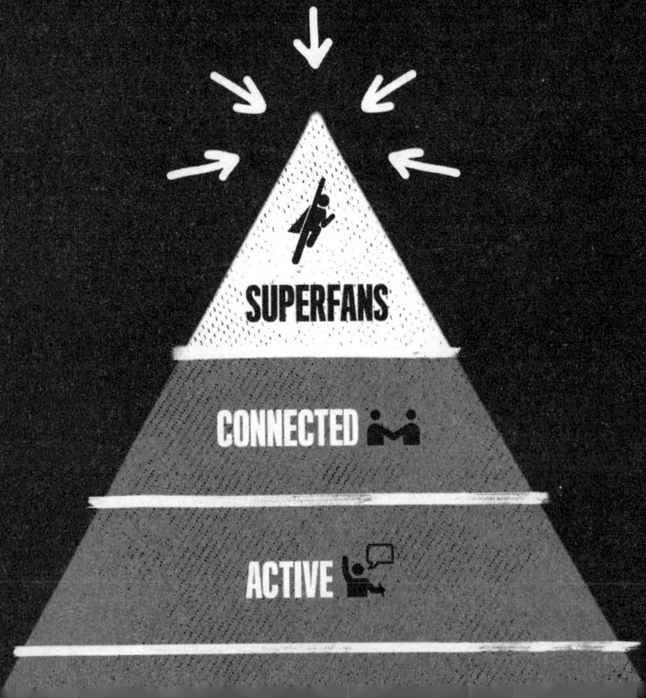

M y superfans have provided me with some of the most positively head-shaking and smile-inducing experiences of my life.

When I came out with my book *Will It Fly?*, one of my fans, a guy named Tom, emailed me and said, "Hey, Pat, I know you're writing this new book. I have no idea what it's about. But you've been so helpful to me, and I'm a big fan. I want to buy twenty copies of your book, and just give it to my friends and family. I don't care what it's about. I know it's going to be helpful because it's you." That blew my mind. A couple other people literally sent me emails with their credit card information and a note saying, "Hey, Pat, when you come out with your next product, I want to buy it. When it's ready, just charge it to me, and send it to me as soon as you can." Incredible, right? The credit card part was a little unsafe, and probably not the smartest thing to do, and I did suggest they not do it again. But it was also very flattering, and a testament to the power of having superfans.

Or take 2010, not long after I launched the *SPI Podcast*, when I got my first group of haters—trolls who got a kick out of saying some really nasty things on my blog. Without being asked, my superfans came to my defense. Many of them also took the time to reach out to me and make sure I was okay. That's the thing about superfans. They'll look out for you. They feel like they know you, that they're part of your brand and your mission. That in a way they share responsibility for you. They want to protect what you've created so that it can continue to help others the way it's helped them.

There was also my experience attending conferences after I started developing a high profile, where people would come up to me and say, "Dude, I listen to you all the time. And now I'm meeting you!" That kind of attention felt weird the first time it happened, and it's *still* weird because I don't feel like a rockstar. That's not to say I'm not thankful for it, because I am, but it's so cool to see that I can have such an impact on a person's life that they're jazzed to meet me in person. Or that someone I've never met will see *Back to the Future* playing on television, then tweet at me because it reminded them of me.

Building a core of superfans is the best way to make your business future proof. As the world changes, as technology evolves, and even as your entrepreneurial path takes its own turns, by focusing on creating special moments that make people feel valued, connected, and celebrated, you're going to win no matter what.

I believe the best and most lasting businesses are the ones that focus on serving first. Money is important, but guess what? At its best, money is simply an amazing byproduct of building a small but potent set of superfans. You don't need millions of dollars, or millions of people following you to build a successful business and lead a successful life. You just need a core group of raving fans who will follow you wherever you go.

If you're a solo entrepreneur or run a small business and one thousand true fans still sounds like a lot to you, remember: that's one fan a day for less than three years. Anyone can provide an amazing experience for one new person every day, and it's your consistency of focusing on those experiences that will lead to building a core group of superfans. Use your size to your advantage to make true connections with people and create unique, memorable moments for them. As Kevin Kelly says, you don't need a huge audience to do some really amazing things, or to change your life and the lives of many others.

If your business is a little bigger, I encourage you to get more ambitious with the experiences you provide for your fans. Use events and community-building exercises like meetups and even live gigs and conferences to bring your community together and foster connections between your brand and your audience, as well as within your audience.

And if your business is a lot bigger—like a Fortune 500 company—use your bigger platform and deeper pockets to reach larger numbers of potential superfans. Open your factory doors and give your audience VIP experiences they'll remember for life.

No matter your size, you can also use your following to help serve the community outside of the arena of your brand, to move your superfans to make positive change in the world. Think of Toms Shoes, a company that donates a pair of shoes with every purchase to kids around the world who need them. Or athletes who give back to their communities. Or SPI, which has supported Pencils of Promise, an organization that has built two schools in Ghana with our help; the SPI community is even mentioned on a plaque at one of those schools.

With superfans on your side, you strengthen your ability to serve the wider community; you have more ways, more support, more energy at your disposal to serve a much greater number of people and causes. Through SPI and its superfans, I've been able to serve in ways I never considered possible.

Your fans want to feel like they're making an impact and are part of something bigger than themselves. When you facilitate and make that happen, you can make great change and service happen, and strengthen those superfan bonds in the process.

If you've made it this far, and you're excited by what you've learned and ready to start cultivating your own band of superfans, I'm not about to leave you hanging. I've created a companion course for the book, titled—wait for it—the Superfans Bonus Companion Course. This free chapter-by-chapter course features bonuses and supplemental materials, including downloadables and videos, that will help you enhance your reading experience with *Superfans* and implement what you learn even faster. Visit yoursuperfans.com/course to get instant access.

I've built my whole brand around the idea of helping people build thriving online businesses by serving their audiences ethically and authentically. My whole philosophy—and all the content I create through SPI, including my blog, podcasts, courses, videos—is geared around serving others. So, if you're curious to continue learning how to create a passive-income-driven online business supported by a cadre of undying superfans, then head over to smartpassiveincome.com, where you'll find all the resources I've created and collected (and continue to do so!) for the past decade-plus.

I wrote this book to help you see that you have the power to make connections with people and create special moments that will endear them to you and your brand for life. Without a bunch of fancy tools or tricks or money for Facebook ads.

I realize you may not consider yourself or your business superfan worthy, but as long as you're guided by an ethic of service, achieving this kind of following is definitely within reach. You'll know you're worthy when you make the mindset shift that *it's not about you*. It's about your audience.

And when you put that mindset into action, people will resonate with you, your message, and the way you do things. Most people won't—and that's okay. Remember that you shouldn't try to make everyone a superfan. If you do, you'll end up diluting your message and your brand and wasting your energy. But if you follow the strategies in this book and realize that you don't need a huge band of superfans to make a difference, enough of the people you connect with *will* take the leap to superfan status—and big time.

Those are the people who are going to lift you up, who you'll be thinking about when you're creating content and designing products and services. They're the people who will help you out when you're stuck, and who will set you straight when you take a wrong turn. They're the ones who will help shape what your brand will become.

As Dale Carnegie said, "The rare individual who unselfishly tries to serve others has an enormous advantage."[16] The beautiful thing is that when you create a legion of loyal superfans by serving people, this enormous advantage doesn't come at a disadvantage to anyone else.

So go do some superfan-making things. Learn the names of your first ten email subscribers and send them an individual note thanking them for joining your list. Put on a live event and feature your most active and dedicated audience members. Give away prizes to a random group of fans without making them enter anything first. Above all, use your handwriting and find your own creative ways to surprise and delight your best fans.

And when you have your own superfan stories to tell, I want to hear them! Share them with me at pat@smartpassiveincome.com, or on Twitter and Instagram (@patflynn). I thrive on hearing from people about the ways they've applied an ethic of service, along with the strategies I've shared in this book, to surprise and delight their own audiences. And be sure to use the hashtag #SuperFansBook!

You can cultivate superfans in many ways, and people will take different paths toward their own version of superfandom. But above all, I promise you, no matter your industry or niche, if you're just getting started or have been in business for ten years: this is possible.

Your future superfans are waiting for you. Go get 'em.

#TeamFlynnForTheWin

---

[16] Dale Carnegie, *How to Win Friends and Influence People*, Reissue edition (Simon & Schuster, 2010), 42.

SUPERFANS BONUS COMPANION COURSE

All of the chapters in this book include exercises to help you engage and interact with your audience in a way that will motivate them to continue on their journey, moving up the Pyramid of Fandom. To get the most out of this book, you might find it helpful to keep track of your ideas and your progress in an organized way.

Although it's not required, I highly recommend you access the free companion course that I've created for you, which you can access at yoursuperfans.com/course.

In this free course, you'll get access to supplemental material including PDF downloads and video instructions. The materials in the course are organized by the sections and chapters of the book, which makes it easy for you to find what you need as you read along.

Visit the following link to get free access to your *Superfans* bonus materials now and I'll see you inside!

yoursuperfans.com/course

THE PODCAST CHEAT SHEET

More than any other platform, my podcast—the *Smart Passive Income Podcast*—has helped me build my audience and foster my own superfans. If you're looking for a no-nonsense guide to get started with podcasting, I've created a resource just for you.

Built on my experience with my own podcast, and helping thousands of people create their own show, my Podcast Cheat Sheet is a start-to-finish checklist that gives you everything you need to launch and succeed with your own podcast.

Visit the URL below to grab the Podcast Cheat Sheet for free:

yoursuperfans.com/podcastcheatsheet

RESOURCES

Here's a list of books, articles, and tools that I've referenced throughout this book:

"1,000 True Fans,"
Original superfans article by Kevin Kelly
kk.org/thetechnium/1000-true-fans

Ask: The Counterintuitive Online Method to Discover Exactly What Your Customers Want to Buy...Create a Mass of Raving Fans...and Take Any Business to the Next Level
Ryan Levesque

I Will Teach You to Be Rich: No Guilt. No B.S. Just a 6-Week Program that Works.
Ramit Sethi

The Power of Habit: Why We Do What We Do In Life and Business
Charles Duhigg

Atomic Habits: An Easy & Proven Way to Build Good Habits & Break Bad Ones
James Clear

0 to 100 Email Challenge
My three-day email list-building challenge
100emails.com

The Social Media Marketing Podcast
Hosted by Michael Stelzner
socialmediaexaminer.com/shows

Amy Porterfield
Online marketing expert
amyporterfield.com

National Novel Writing Month
nanowrimo.org

Pro Blogger
Tips to help you make money blogging
problogger.net

Marketing Impact Academy and Smart Success Seminar
Chalene Johnson's events
chalenejohnson.com

Entrepreneurs on Fire
Podcast hosted by John Lee Dumas
eofire.com

The Tipping Point: How Little Things Can Make a Big Difference
Malcolm Gladwell

Harness Your ADHD Power Podcast
Hosted by Dr. B.
harnessyouradhdpower.com

Epic Success Podcast
Hosted by Dr. Shannon Irvine
drshannonirvine.com/podcast/

Disney Travel Secrets
Podcast hosted by Rob and Kerri Stuart
disneytravelsecrets.mykajabi.com/blog

Mind Love
Podcast hosted by Melissa Monte
mindlove.com

How to Win Friends and Influence People
Dale Carnegie

Bonjoro
The world's first customer delight platform
bonjoro.com

ConvertKit
My preferred email service provider
convertkit.com

Podfest Expo
Multimedia podcasting expo where I've been both an attendee and speaker
podfestexpo.com

Podcast Movement
Podcast tradeshow and festival where I've also been both an attendee and speaker
podcastmovement.com

The Walker Stalkers Podcast **and Walker Stalker Con**
thewalkerstalkers.com

The Sleep Revolution: Transforming Your Life, One Night at A Time
Arianna Huffington

Sleep Smarter: 21 Essential Strategies to Sleep Your Way to a Better Body, Better Health, and Bigger Success
Shawn Stevenson

LET GO: MY UNEXPECTED PATH FROM PANIC TO PROFITS AND PURPOSE

Let Go is Pat Flynn's personal story of overcoming adversity through a commitment to pursuing his own path. When a job layoff in a bad economy forced Pat to reconsider his career as an architect, he found an unexpected path forward. Along the way, he managed to not only achieve financial success, but more importantly discovered what matters most: passion and purpose.

In *Let Go*, Pat reveals the inside story of his transformation into one of today's most beloved thought leaders in the areas of internet business, online marketing, and lifestyle entrepreneurialism. He shares the challenges and feelings he faced as he pieced together what has become a thriving online enterprise.

This book has evolved over time, beginning as a blog post in 2012 and expanding into a Kindle book in 2013. In 2018, Pat published an expanded edition with more stories and lessons learned since becoming a successful entrepreneur—because the truth is that he's had to learn to let go of even more to grow his business and raise a family.

If you share Pat's impulse to pursue your own path, then you'll enjoy reading *Let Go*. After all, we all must confront the same risky idea if we are to unlock our true potential: letting go.

yoursuperfans.com/letgo

Will It Fly?

HOW TO TEST YOUR NEXT BUSINESS IDEA SO YOU DON'T WASTE YOUR TIME AND MONEY

Wall Street Journal bestseller *Will It Fly?* is a series of tests to prove that your business idea has wings. Chock-full of practical suggestions you can apply to your business idea today, *Will It Fly?* combines action-based exercises, small-scale litmus tests, and real-world case studies. These tests will help you answer these questions:

- Does your business idea have merit?
- Does your idea fit the market you want to serve?
- Is your idea a good fit for you and the kind of business you want to run?

Think of this book as your business flight manual, something you can refer to for honest and straightforward advice as you begin to test your idea and build a business that takes off and soars.

Will It Fly? covers five parts:

- **Part One: Mission Design** helps you make sure your target idea aligns with and supports your goals.
- **Part Two: Development Lab** walks you through uncovering important details about your idea that you haven't even thought about.
- **Part Three: Flight Planning** is all about assessing current market conditions.
- **Part Four: Flight Simulator** focuses on the actual validating and testing of an idea with a small segment of a target market.
- **Part Five: All Systems Go** is for final analysis to help you make sure your idea is one you are ready to move forward with.

Get your copy of *Will It Fly?* at this link:

yoursuperfans.com/willitfly

ACKNOWLEDGMENTS

It would double the size of the book if I were to thank every single person who has had an impact on making this book a reality. Truly. From every single supporting member of #TeamFlynn, to the doubters and trolls who have tried to take me down (yet, have only made me stronger), thank you. I will, however, mention a few specific names, because without these amazing people, this book would not exist.

First, I want to thank my wife, April. If it weren't for two things: her undying love for the Backstreet Boys and her incredible support of me and my business, none of this would be here. And I'm not just talking about *Superfans*, but my entire business. As a stay-at-home parent, she has one of the hardest jobs in the world—one that comes with no pay and hardly any recognition, and requires a 24/7, 365 commitment—and yet she still encourages me and rallies behind my wins along the way. She's an incredible mother and a loving wife, and I'm so thankful to have her in my life (even though I'm an N'Sync fan).

Second, I'd like to thank my kids, Keoni and Kailani. They inspire me every day to be the best version of myself and to set the best example I can for their future. Although I want them to be kids forever, I'm excited to see how they grow and use the lessons they learn from my work as an entrepreneur, and my wife's work as a stay-at-home mom, to shape their future. I will forever be a superfan of their curiosity for how things work, and their empathy for others.

I'm also a huge superfan of Team SPI, the amazing crew of people who keep SmartPassiveIncome.com running smoothly—mostly behind the scenes. Matt Gartland, my COO and CFO, is a lot more than just a bunch of important acronyms. He's a dear friend and a true visionary who is a whiz with spreadsheets, and I'm excited to see just what kind of impact we can make on this world together.

A big thanks, too, to Janna Maron, our Content Director. She's also known as "The Whipcracker" on the team because she's always on us if we don't meet our deadlines! She's helped to keep everyone on task, and on schedule—and for an undertaking like *Superfans*, with so many moving parts and pieces, that's extremely important. Then there's Jess Lindgren, my executive assistant, who has helped keep me sane during this entire process. Thanks to Mindy Holahan, Ray Sylvester, Non Wels, Karen Beattie, Sara Jane Hess, Dustin Tevis, Caleb Wojcik, and the team over at New Type Publishing for helping with all aspects of bringing this book to life.

Additionally, I'd like to give a shout out to Jay Baer, who, one day after I presented on the topic of raving fans, said I should turn that content into a book—and now here we are. Thank you to Michael Stelzner, for allowing me to keynote Social Media Marketing World in 2018 in front of five thousand people, which validated some of the content in this book, and a thank you to the other members of the Green Room mastermind: Cliff Ravenscraft, Leslie Samuel, Mark Mason, and Ray Edwards. Also thank you to Jaime Masters, Shawn Stevenson, Todd Tressider, and Rosemarie Groner, who are in another mastermind group with me; Chris Ducker, my best friend, for inspiring me and leading the way with publishing his own flagship book recently, *Rise of the Youpreneur*; and Michael Hyatt and Chalene Johnson, for being mentors and role models.

Seriously, there are way too many people to thank for this book—I have to stop here, or else I never will. But one more—and that's you— the reader of *Superfans*. Thank you not only for reading this book, but also for taking action. Remember: it just takes one fan a day, and soon enough, you'll start to see your name show up when your fans acknowledge who has helped them along the way. Here's to you and your future success.

Team Flynn for the win!

ABOUT SMART PASSIVE INCOME (SPI)

Smart Passive Income (smartpassiveincome.com) is a resource run by Pat Flynn that teaches individuals how to start and run a successful online business. The site includes step-by-step advice for building, launching, and growing an online business. SPI is dedicated to providing ethical business advice that has been properly tested.

SPI includes a variety of free resources to assist you:

The SPI blog contains detailed, step-by-step advice and strategies for each stage of your business, as well as in-depth reviews of tools and resources.

The Smart Passive Income Podcast is a weekly, top-ranked podcast with expert interviews and reader success stories.

AskPat is a weekly podcast where Pat dives deep with one entrepreneur on a targeted coaching call that addresses their most critical business questions.

Pat's **YouTube channel** is where he explores and guides viewers through the world of passive income and online business building, including tips and tutorials, interviews, and even the occasional home office tour.

Thanks for reading this book! By now you're hopefully making awesome progress building your own set of superfans.

Let's keep in touch—join the SPI email list for free business advice and encouragement as you help your audience members ascend the Pyramid of Fandom.

Go to yoursuperfans.com/thankyou to sign up. You'll get periodic advice on strategies for building your business and fanbase, recommendations (and the occasional discount) on useful tools I've tested, and case studies from entrepreneurs just like you who have built online businesses and raving audiences of their own.

I can't wait to see what you can do!

yoursuperfans.com/thankyou

ABOUT THE AUTHOR

PAT FLYNN is a popular podcaster, author, and founder of several successful websites, including Smart Passive Income, where he helps people build thriving online businesses. He has been featured in *Forbes* and in the *New York Times* for his work. He calls himself the "Crash Test Dummy of Online Business" because he loves to put himself on the line and experiment with various business strategies so that he can report his findings publicly to his audience. He's also the author of two other books: *Let Go,* a memoir about his transition from architecture into entrepreneurship, and *Will It Fly?*, a business book about how to validate ideas before investing too many resources. He speaks on the topics of product validation, audience engagement, and personal branding.

Pat is also an advisor to Pencils of Promise, a nonprofit organization dedicated to building schools in the developing world. Pat lives in San Diego with his wife, April, and their two children.

To learn more about Pat go to:
smartpassiveincome.com/about.